A Chance to Change

Women and Men in the Church

BETTY THOMPSON

Fortress Press
Philadelphia, Pa.

World Council of Churches
Geneva, Switzerland

For
John P. Taylor
1920–1982
Partner in the Community

First Fortress Press Edition 1982

Library of Congress Cataloging in Publication Data

Thompson, Betty.
  A chance to change.

  Bibliography: p.
  1. Man (Theology) 2. Thompson, Betty. I. Title.
BT701.2.T484 1982   262'.7   82-71832
ISBN 0-8006-1645-6

9592E82   Printed in the United States of America   1–1645

Contents

Preface—A Word to the Consumer 5

"Think on These Things" 7
  —Mercy Oduyoye, *Nigeria*

Introduction—Ever Since Eve 9

1. A Chance to Change 15

2. Process, Pain, and Risk 21

"Human Being" 31
  —Maen Pongudom, *Thailand*

3. Becoming Human in the New Community 32

4. From Pyramid to Circle 41

"Dear Mother Church" 48
  —Margaret Davies, *Great Britain*

5. A Home for Humanity 50

6. Scripture in the New Community 59

"The Name of God" 68
  —Elizabeth Streefland, *The Netherlands*

7. The Third World Speaks Out 71

8. Beyond Sheffield 82

9. Reality to the Vision 90

"Women in Exodus Commune with God" 102
  —Helen Schmidt, *Germany*

A Letter from Sheffield 105

Notes 108

Bibliography 111

photo by John Goodwin

Preface
A Word to the Consumer

This book is based on the World Council of Churches study on the Community of Women and Men in the Church and the consultation held in Sheffield, England, on that subject in the summer of 1981. It is an attempt to share and enlarge the discussion on the subject. To that end it mixes material from the preliminary studies, speeches and findings of the conference, and subsequent actions. It is no linear blow-by-blow diary of a meeting. It does not cover in meticulous detail every major address or include every word of the section reports and recommendations. That book, admirably edited by the director of the study, Constance Parvey, is the official report, *The Community of Women and Men in the Church* (Fortress Press, 1983). It is not a history of the women's department in the World Council of Churches. That book is *A Voice for Women* by Susannah Herzel. I commend both of these volumes for those who wish to go deeper into the questions raised here.

Nor is this book an official World Council of Churches document signed with the Oikumene Seal of Approval. It does appear in the WCC Risk Series as well as in the United States under the imprint of Fortress Press. But it does not carry the imprimatur of an official document. It was commissioned by the World Council with the understanding that, as with the series in which it is published, risk is involved. Although I have worked for the World Council of Churches and served on its communications advisory committee, the choice of material, its arrangement, and prejudices expressed here are mine. The findings of the conference have already been the subject of some debate in the World Council.

I write as a journalist, a North American lay woman in a tradition which ordains women and has elected its first woman bishop only recently. Therefore, I come with a bias. I have been very fortunate in my ecumenical encounters over a quarter of a century. Ultimately we select and order our material out of our own experiences and belief. As far as possible I have let the material speak for itself.

My thanks go especially to Constance Parvey, who looked ever so lightly over my shoulder but did not see the final manuscript before it went to the printer. I also want to thank her predecessors on the journey, Madeline Barot and Brigalia Bam, for doing what we now call raising consciousness in me. I am aware that the women of United Methodism in the generations just behind me furnished what some of them would be astonished to hear called role models.

I am grateful to the Board of Global Ministries of the United Methodist Church for giving me a sabbatical and allowing me to take it at intervals which enabled the completion of this book. To all who have struggled with my typing and handwriting, which have been accused of looking more like a ransom note than a manuscript, I give thanks. Brenda Wilkinson, herself a gifted writer, is chief among these. And, a special word of gratitude to my friend Jo-Ann Price Baehr, journalist and photographer, who generously shared her notes and her photographs.

Betty Thompson
New York
Easter 1982

Think on These Things

Wake up, my soul, and bless the Lord.
The whole creation blesses the Lord
The earth and the sky sing together
And oceans and seas reply
The continents and islands clap their hands,
and the shores of Ayia Napa are filled
with the joyful splashes of morning swimmers
The flowers and the birds wake up with the sun;
Wake up, my soul, and bless the Lord.

The joyful sounds of pots and pans
the coffee, the tea bags and the sugar bowl
bow together.
The clang of cups and spoons sing praise
in anticipation of breaking the long fast.
The cheese, the milk and the egg
fish, meat and salad, wine and good cold water
Wake up, my soul, and bless the Lord.

Announce the Holy Spirit reigns in the monastery
For the active participation of presidents
and cooks, travel agents and shopkeepers;
For the self-emptying of stewards and secretaries,
For meticulous administrators and careful drivers.
For bankers, house-keepers and road menders
For the courage of all the wananki and minjung of this world
Wake up, my soul, and bless the Lord.

For those who structure or moderate
For those who tell stories and those who listen
For those who draft and those who analyze
For all legitimate steering and helpful history
For every thought noble and lofty
Creation and Fall, Cross and Resurrection.

For Koinonia, Trinity and Incarnation
And every word of good news to the poor.
For the ethics of our participation
and every intention to turn to justice and to truth
Wake up, my soul, and bless the Lord.

The whole consultation blesses the Lord
Issues of Justice, and Power, the matter
of the people and their participation,
The blank sheet of sustainability and
the simple question of ecumenical political ethics.
The people around the table are blessing the
Lord—wake up! bless the Lord for
participation vertical and horizontal
for equality in the political area
For dialogue between theology and zoology
for the active presence of creatures great and small;
For the song and dance, the words and the wit
Wake up, my soul, and bless the Lord.

No more the Saturday feeling
No more the walk on Desolation Road
No more the waiting for Resurrection
It HAPPENED 2,000 years ago!
Wake up, my soul, and bless the Lord
The Anointed of the Lord walks among
THE PEOPLE.

Mercy Oduyoye
Nigeria

Introduction
Ever Since Eve

So God created man in his own image, in the image of God he created him: male and female he created them.

Gen. 1:27

For as many of you as were baptized into Christ have put on Christ. There is neither Jew nor Gentile, there is neither slave nor free, there is neither male nor female; for you are all one in Christ.

Gal. 3:27–28

Both male and female are created in the image of God—*imago dei*—so the first creation account in Genesis tells us. And St. Paul assured the Galatians that in Christ there are no gender superiorities. Jesus himself put a high value on women in all of his ministry. So why is the Christian church considered by many to be not only an oppressive, male-dominated institution but also, according to some Asian and African observers, even more oppressive than earlier cultures and religions?

Turn to Genesis 2 and find another account of the creation of men and women. From the first-created sleeping male, the Lord God took a rib and made woman. And the same Paul, writing to the Ephesians, described man as the head of the wife and Christ as head of the church: "As the Church is subject to Christ, so let wives also be subject in everything to their husbands." He advised the Corinthians that women should keep silent in the churches and if they desired to know anything, to ask their husbands. Jesus chose twelve men as his disciples, thus giving rise to the tradition that only men are to be priests.

For nearly 2,000 years the primacy of man in church and society has been accepted. Man as priest, preacher, papa, pope seemed right and normal. Woman was helpmeet, mother, homekeeper, and silence keeper. How do we interpret the Genesis story? To which words of St. Paul do we listen, and do we understand the circumstances of the

9

churches to which he was writing and his own religious and cultural background? Are we selective about the examples of Jesus' behavior to women that we cite? These and scores of other questions about Scripture, tradition, authority, and structure have been the focus of studies by tens of thousands of women and men around the world in the period between the Fifth Assembly of the World Council of Churches in Nairobi, Kenya, in 1975, and the Sixth Assembly in Vancouver, Canada, in 1983.

This book attempts to sketch the history of this issue in the modern ecumenical movement and to describe the international consultation held in Sheffield, England, in 1981 as it looked at the future of the community of women and men in the church. Because the issues are ancient and the views many, this volume can only touch upon the problems and opportunities facing the church today. It is intended to introduce the subject to a wider audience and to be part of the initiation of a dialogue in the churches which will find its way into the Vancouver assembly and the life of the churches. The Rev. Dr. Philip Potter, the general secretary of the World Council of Churches, reminded us at Sheffield that as far back as 1927, at the Lausanne Conference on Faith and Order, there were seven women among the hundreds of men who gathered to discuss the unity of the church. These women had the courage to say ''that the right place of women in the church is a matter of grave moment and should be in the minds and hearts of all.'' That, observed Potter, was the polite language of the time. They also reminded the church fathers that if the churches were seeking deeper unity they would have to reexamine the question of relationships between women and men.

''Ready as usual, the churches repeated these phrases for several years until we met together for the inauguration of the World Council of Churches in 1948 (in Amsterdam). At that first assembly we declared that the Church as the Body of Christ consists of men and women created as responsible persons to glorify God and to do His will. And the statement immediately went on to say, 'This truth accepted in theory is too often ignored in practice.' ''

When I joined the staff of the World Council of Churches in Geneva in 1955, just a year after the Second Assembly in

Evanston, Illinois, there were only a half-dozen women executives (none of them at top level) although, as in most organizations, there were scores in the lower echelons of secretaries, translators, and assistants who made the thing work. One of those executive women was Madeline Barot, who headed an operation called the Cooperation of Men and Women in Church and Society. Madeline appeared to be chiefly admired for her work as a Resistance heroine in World War II who had helped form the refugee and relief organization Cimade and spirited Jewish children over the border to Switzerland during Nazi days. This "Napoleon in skirts," as she was called by some of her male colleagues, was rumored to be responsible for mysterious papers on the gender of the Almighty and the sex of angels. Actually Madeline's work came out of a solid survey of the role of women in the churches undertaken prior to the first assembly. It was this documentation of the lowly place of women in the ecclesiastical scheme that accounted for the mild tremor of recognition to be found in the Amsterdam reports. A brilliant Anglican woman, Kathleen Bliss, one of the first women to serve on the World Council's Executive Committee, wrote a report based on the survey on "The Role and Status of Men and Women in Church." By 1954, the Office of Cooperation of Men and Women had been established in Geneva and Madeline called to head it. An advisory committee was set up to guide the office which produced theological papers, held consultations, established a global network, especially of women, and kept the issue alive in the churches.

The modern ecumenical movement dates from the 1910 Edinburgh Conference on the World Mission of the Church. One seeks in vain in the pictures of these early conferences for any women, yet women missionaries and women's missionary organizations were powerful influences in the latter part of the nineteenth and early part of the twentieth centuries. These organizations were set up because men refused women any participation in the mission movement but that of raising funds. The Life and Work movement and the Faith and Order movement were the other tributaries of the ecumenical stream that came together in the immediate postwar world to form a permanent World Council of

Churches. One also searches in vain for speeches by women or even attendance by women in the predecessor organizations of the Council.

After the Amsterdam Assembly, the World Council set up an official Commission of the Life and World of Women in the Church. An Indian educator, Sarah Chakko, was appointed chairperson and Kathleen Bliss was appointed secretary. In 1950 Miss Chakko had taken a sabbatical from her duties as the head of Isabella Thoburn College and spent more than a year working full-time for the commission. When the Chinese president of the World Council of Churches resigned in 1951, Sarah Chakko was chosen to succeed him and thus became the first woman to serve on the Council presidium. She died in 1954. It was not until 1968 that another woman was chosen for the six-person presidium; again an Asian, Dr. Kiyoko Takeda Cho of Japan.

Because of the structure of the churches, the overwhelming majority of the policy makers of the new council were men. On the powerful Central Committee that guided the Council between assemblies, the heads of the churches (often bishops, archbishops, metropolitans, moderators, stated clerks, and the like) were seated. By the time of the Third Assembly at New Delhi, India, in 1961, there were a score of women out of the 900 delegates appointed by the member churches. The World Christian Student Movement and the World Young Women's Christian Association were the primary training grounds for women, but as the Council took on an inevitable ecclesiastical character, the chances for female participation were even less.

At the Uppsala Assembly in Sweden in 1968, the various movements for justice were making an impact on the church. Barbara Ward was a speaker there. Margaret Mead had taken a key role in the 1966 World Conference on Church and Society (another largely-male group) and was present at Uppsala. Uppsala was conscious of race and of the struggle for economic justice in the developing world but little formal attention was paid to sexism. When women delegates were invited to stand up at some point in the proceedings, it was apparent how few were there (about nine percent).

By 1975, when the World Council's Fifth Assembly took place in Nairobi, Kenya, an entire session of the assembly was given over to the concerns of women. A major conference had been held in 1974 in Berlin on the subject of sexism. The climate at Nairobi was very different from previous World Council assemblies. Both at the plenary on "Women in a Changing World" and in the sections the impact of their concern was felt. When the World Council chose its six honorary presidents, two women were among them—Justice Annie Jiagge, a Presbyterian from Ghana, and Mrs. Cynthia Wedel, an Episcopalian from the United States.

At Nairobi the group dealing with structures of injustice recommended a three-year study on the Community of Women and Men in the Church. So the process was set in motion that was to involve a greater number of persons than any previous World Council study. It was to last four years, not three, and to culminate in a consultation held in Sheffield in 1981.

The Community of Women and Men in the Church is not just a subject for theological debate at global assemblies. This study has come out of the reality of local churches on every continent. It is no longer a "for women only" issue but a concern for every witnessing community.

Participants in the World Council of Churches Assembly in Nairobi

photo by John Taylor

1

A Chance to Change

It was the summer of 1981. England presented two faces to the world. The happy one was preoccupied with arrangements for the royal wedding. The future king was taking a bride. Shop windows were filled with pictures of the radiant couple and piled high with souvenirs made in Hong Kong or other outposts of the former empire. But beneath the festive facade, there was another face: troubled, angry, frightened. This was the England of unemployment and riots, of broken shop windows, and roaming gangs of unemployed youth.

Participants in the international consultation on Women and Men in the Church, held on the campus of the University of Sheffield, July 10–20, 1981, were largely insulated from both the euphoria of the romantic myth and the gravity of Western industrial democracy's painful winding down. Like so many other global conclaves, Sheffield (the conferences ultimately come to be known by the names of the cities which host them), though it spoke the rhetoric of international concern, could as well have been in any other place.

The two hundred men and women who came to the conference from fifty countries lived that special, somewhat artificial life of the ecumenical event. They had never been together before as a community of people and would never in time exist again in just the same configuration. For a little more than a week, delegates from one hundred churches were housed, fed, and transported together. Those staples of the World Council of Churches conferences—documentation and simultaneous translation—helped bridge their linguistic and other differences.

We were the usual ecclesiastical hodgepodge: a mixture of enthusiasts for the subject augmented by persons trusted by our churches to be official delegates, young men and women working as volunteers or stewards, observers, "experts," translators, secretaries, and the usual motley crew of press to which I belonged. As I wearily slung my luggage into the dignified, unchanging British black taxicab at the railway station, the usual mixture of anticipation and apprehension I have experienced at so many church meetings filled me. Is this trip necessary? Will anyone really be changed? Will the recommendations be heeded, and will they have any effect on the member churches? Are the expenditures merited? Has this kind of conference, characteristic of the modern ecumenical movement, had its day? I flinched at the intellectual group grope as we tried to find some understanding across our cultural and theological differences. But mingled with all these thoughts and stronger than fear was the hope that once more out of all the clumsiness of our process something fresh would emerge.

Not all the participants shared my ecumenical ennui. One of the heartening things I observed at the registration desk and in the dining hall was the dearth of familiar faces. This was not the old gang but a group of persons with many first-time participants in a World Council of Churches conference. Another striking thing was that women outnumbered men about three to one. As a veteran of three World Council assemblies, a former staff member of the Council, and one who belongs to one of its advisory committees, I was accustomed to being in the definite gender minority. Here the situation was reversed. I wondered if the men present felt as I had sometimes felt, outnumbered and a bit out of place. Another change was the large number of delegates from Africa, Latin America, Asia, and the islands of the Pacific and the Caribbean.

Arriving a bit late at a conference has advantages as well as disadvantages. You have to be especially alert to try to catch up. The tendency is to think anyone with a 24-hour advantage is far ahead of you in understanding and a feeling of community. By my arrival on Sunday, the participants had already been dispersed to local churches in the Sheffield area and were full of stories of the warmth with which they had been received. This visitation in the churches and the formal but very warm hospitality extended by the lady mayor at a dinner at the Town Hall the following evening were the primary links with the local community. The bishop of Sheffield opened his home to those who wished to come on subsequent evenings. A local feminist group visited the conference site and met informally with those who were interested. Stewards organized a visit to the troubled Moss Side area of Liverpool and the Sheffield Industrial Mission invited members of the group to hear about its work. Sheffield area residents were kept informed about the conference by an excellent local British Broadcasting Corporation reporter. Despite these efforts, the majority of residents in the area had little idea of what was going on at Earnshaw Hall, the residential college where we were housed, or on the university campus proper in the red brick Victorian Firth Hall, or in the modern high-rise Arts Towers where the meetings were held.

"Women in Pulpit Will Have More Sex Appeal for Men" was the story carried round the world by wire services as the main coverage of this meeting. As so often in the reporting of meetings having to do with sexism, sensational and false accounts occur. The alternative seems to be to ignore the meeting altogether. Sheffield was a victim of both of these media distortions. The sensational reporting based on an interview with a local participant appeared in no less august a place than the *Times* of London.

Dr. Philip Potter, the general secretary of the World Council of Churches, stated the agenda simply and forcefully in his address to the conference. "What then is our agenda here?" the Caribbean churchman asked. "It is to consider the issues of liberation from sexism, the systematic, historical, and present subordination of women by men, and their liberation for a truly human life as a community of women and men in church and society."

By sharing what he himself had learned from the study thus far, Dr. Potter gave great hope and encouragement to the gathering. Reading between the lines as an old "ecumeniac," the chief executive of the World Council acknowledged that reports are only a kind of algebraic sign of a great depth of buried meaning. "What I have learned from this decoding exercise is that compared, for example, with the anger and frustration of the 1974 Berlin Conference on Sexism [held by WCC], I felt here through this enormous study, which has gone on in so many parts of the world, the incredible pain and agony of it all, and with it the extraordinary love and patient endurance and perseverance which lie behind it."

To Potter the reports brought an awareness of the tremendous insight and wisdom of women which have been "lying there wasted for so many years and which are still emerging, thank God, for our enrichment. I have been aware reading these reports of the impotence of our male-dominated churches to see, hear, feel, decide, and act. And incensed with this impotence, I wait for the potency which God's spirit can bring to us."

It was obvious that this speech was no formal, bureaucratic necessity but a heartfelt cry of conviction from the general secretary. "For me, this study is a veritable test of our faith and of the ecumenical movement which is concerned about the unity of the whole people of God as a sign and sacrament of the unity of all the people of the world . . ." Speaking personally again, Potter said that what emerged most powerfully for him was the need to rethink the whole question of authority and interpretation of Scripture. Even more than in the issues of racism and social injustice, he finds the way in which the relations of men and women have been dealt with in the Scriptures brings into question how we understand the total revelation of God in Christ expressed in Scripture. The result, he says, is that we have systematically left aside as our criterion of judgment "the central nature of God's revelation and clung to all the things that confirm and strengthen our attitudes of domination and of hierarchical oppression."

The second big impact the study had for Potter was in terms of ecclesiology. "Our understanding of the church, the 'laos,' the laity, the whole people of God . . . what *do* we mean when we speak of the church as the 'whole people of God'? . . . What does it mean for the way the church functions? If there is a fellowship, a real sharing life, then it means both women and men are in the World Council together, that decisions are made by whoever has the gifts regardless of sex or culture."

During Potter's administration a woman was vice-chair of the Central Committee, the powerful policy-making body, and the presidium has two honorary women presidents. He remarks that the tendency in the church has been to turn the word "ministry," which means being servant, into hierarchy or patriarchy. "We know that the servant is the one who empties him or herself, not seeking to have power and domination." And he observed that the servant church had set up all kinds of individual and corporate forms of hierarchy that enshrine power attitudes and structures.

Another area which troubled Dr. Potter was the understanding of Tradition and traditions. As a student of history, he expressed the desire to rewrite church history as the history "of women and men in mission and service. Our existing history is largely a history of men." He recounts an incident when he was preparing for a visit from the patriarch of the Orthodox Church of Georgia in the Soviet Union. In the course of boning up he discovered in his library research that the first missionary to that church was St. Nina, in the fourth century. "It was Queen Bertha who gave land to St. Augustine and his followers, the land on which the cathedral of Canterbury was built," he told his audience, which included the archbishop of Canterbury.

In his brief overview of church history, the ecumenical leader affirmed that wherever there were renewal movements in the church they had been led by women. "Consider women prophets in the books they wrote, and combined with mysticism, their active service in the community in the Middle Ages." He cited Quakers and the equality among men and women in that community, the Moravians, and "even the Methodists," according to Methodist minister Potter. "The Methodist movement in the eighteenth century owed a tremendous deal to women all up and down these islands, and indeed in other parts of the world."

"Today all around the world wherever there are renewal movements, base communities who are developing their consciousness and going out and daring the oppressive authorities, there are women in the vanguard," he said. To his historical notes he added the role played by women in the missionary movement and in the ecumenical movements, starting with the Young Women's Christian Association and the Student Christian Movement "in which so many of us men learned how to live with women as equals, only we did not know how to carry it on from there."

Paying tribute to the study for deepening theological understanding of what it means to be human, the general secretary spoke of the heresy of dividing spirit and flesh and attributing spirit to man and flesh to woman. "Or again the dualism of private and public—women being private and men public." And the third dualism being challenged is that of meekness over power—the meekness belongs to women and power to men . . . "Because of the inability to relate these two things, our humanity has been brutalized and we are where we are in pursuit of death by rearmament and war."

The study helped Potter in understanding the central relationship between identity and community. "The heart of God's revelation of humanity was male and female. In that he indicated to us that there is no homogeneous, uniform way by which God wills that we should live, but rather in full recognition of our diversities, and through those diversities we find our unity and community."

Finally, Dr. Potter said the study had given him fresh impetus to our quest for justice and peace. "We have been talking a great deal about development as self-reliance but we haven't noticed that in most of the world, especially the poor world, it's the women who have been carrying the tremendous burden of poverty and self-development. . . . The struggle for peace in a war-obsessed world is only possible when women are deeply and decisively engaged politically."

In his wide ranging and deeply felt speech, Philip Potter broke open many of the subjects which were to engage the conference for the next week. And he put his not inconsiderable weight into the struggle for a true community of women and men in the church and society.

2

Process, Pain, and Risk

Studies, consultations, and reports often appear to come from the air or to have been cloned in some mysterious ecumenical laboratory. But there are always individual women and men who make them happen. They are usually a footnote in the church history books. They are not among those few charismatic leaders whose roles, special gifts, or the accidents of history (or the workings of the Holy Spirit) make them, if not household words, recognizable by the media and other church leaders. We live in an age in which there are few universally recognized Christian person-alities—the pope, a rare Mother Teresa, an occasional evangelist like Billy Graham, a handful of theologians. There appear to be no more Barths or Brunners, Tillichs or Niebuhrs, no widely known martyrs like Bonhoeffer or Martin Luther King, no globally known gifted preachers like D. T. Niles. Notice the dearth of women in this list of recognizable church personalities of the present and im-mediate past ecumenical life. Yet there are many women and men whose unruly vision and hard work create slow miracles.

In reading the 30-year-old study on *The Service and Status of Women in the Churches* by Kathleen Bliss, it is evident that while the same theological arguments are still used against the participation of women in the leadership of the churches and that some churches have not changed at all, the world picture is quite different. Because of the presence of women like Kathleen Bliss herself and the impressive theological and biblical work led by Madeline Barot, the explosion of women's concerns at the 1974 Berlin Conference, led by Brigalia Bam, and the insistence by tens of thousands of women that they share in all the respon-sibilities of church and society, there is a new attitude both among women themselves and toward their participation by men. The single most important change is simply that many, mostly anonymous, women have come to believe "I am because I participate" and they are no longer content to be the silent majority.

Constance Parvey, D.D., Lutheran minister, formerly chaplain to students at Harvard University and Massachusetts Institute of Technology, is the person who more than any other made the idea conceived at the Berlin Conference on Sexism in the 1970s and born at the Nairobi Assembly a reality. Soft-spoken Connie, as she came to be known on all six continents, with a combination of American daring, feminist awareness, and theological conviction, set about the difficult assignment of making an underfinanced and hardly popular theme known throughout the world—in remote communities of Latin America and the Pacific Islands as well as in North American seminaries and European cities. A gentle smile and a loving spirit, coupled with seeming obliviousness to the impossibility of the task or the myriad of details required, enabled Connie to transmit a vision beyond the usual official church level to the towns and villages across the world. At times it looked as though the Sheffield Consultation would never be—no money, no people to organize it, no interest at highest church levels. That it did finally come off is due to Connie's hope and the assistance of the Rev. Janet Crawford, an Anglican priest from New Zealand, who brought her administrative gifts to help organize the multifaceted Sheffield gathering.

Connie tells her own story of the idea in the address to the Asian Consultation held in Bangalore in August of 1978. She told Asian participants that the idea of "the community" study had its origin, its history, in the beginnings of the ecumenical movement and its women leaders, and even further back to those in the nineteenth century who gave importance to the education of women and established women's colleges in India and other parts of the world. Connie's own deep interest began when she attended the Berlin Conference on Sexism. "Many of us had been at world gatherings before, but had never been at a meeting of all women who were our peers from many continents, churches, and professions—education, law, medicine, theology, politics, the social sciences, etc. For many, the Berlin experience was a turning point. We have had numerous occasions to meet with men of similar education and work, but none to meet with other women of our generation to share with them our faith, professions, and hope."

Then pastor of a Lutheran congregation in Cambridge, Massachusetts, where she also was a chaplain to students at Harvard and the Massachusetts Institute of Technology, Connie had been sent by the Lutheran Church in America as an official representative to the Berlin Conference. Asked in good ecumenical fashion to chair a group on politics and women, Connie protested that she knew little about politics and preferred to chair a section on theology, an idea which received a cool response. It was perceived that there would be little interest in theology but the conference leadership assented to her idea and a score of women came to the group. Mostly they were women who had been theologically trained but now worked as teachers, journalists, or in other professions. "Only a few were teaching theology or writing theology, and those mostly from the kitchen sink as they nurtured young children," Connie recalls.

Actually it was from this group that the idea which sparked the community study came into being. "As we shared our stories we discovered that though we were all very serious and committed Christians, we were marginal to the church's institutional life. Few doors were open to us. Most of our contributions to the life and thought of the church had come through our own initiative, and not because we had been involved in church structures. Few in the group were employed by church-related institutions and many expressed difficulty at finding even volunteer work in the church that was meaningful. The group took the refuge of the frustrated; they formulated a recommendation. This was to suggest to the World Council of Churches a study on the implications for theology and church structure of women into new levels of participation in theological reflection, ministry, and church life."

Tracking the journey, Connie followed the idea through the Faith and Order Commission in Accra, Ghana, in 1974 and its emergence from the Nairobi Assembly in 1975 as a major study of the World Council. The 1976 policy-making Central Committee lodged the study in the Faith and Order

Commission with the cooperation of the subunit on women. This recognized two points, according to Connie. The program would not exist without the collaborative reflection of both women and men on the theological and ecclesial (related to the church) issues involved.

Just after Sheffield, in informal observation to the World Council staff executive group, the study director recalled that at the 1976 Central Committee of the WCC, there had been an argument on whether the topic was an issue of unity (Faith and Order) or the liberation of women (the women's department). So both WCC units were engaged in the study, and the realization came from Sheffield that unity and human liberation cannot be separated.

The study was plagued by funding problems from the start. That is not unusual for Council studies, but this one found fewer advocates at the level of the top ecclesiastical types than usual. Women's organizations at the beginning withheld funds for the study because they wished it to be undertaken as a primary responsibility by the churches themselves, not just the women's groups. When funding was secured, Constance Parvey moved from her Cambridge, Massachusetts, parish to Geneva and set about the work of preparing the conference. Originally the international consultation was slated for 1980.

The conference at the United Theological College in Bangalore in August of 1978 was the first of six regional conferences. In 1980 regional consultations were held in Africa, Europe, and the Middle East. In 1981, a Latin American consultation was held and one was held in the United States of America. In addition, three specialized consultations were held in Europe. These were small, "expert" (although this study was less inclined toward academic elitism than most in the World Council), intense study conferences on the ordination of women (Klingenthal), the *imago dei* (Niederaltaich), and the authority of Scripture (Amsterdam).

The specialized consultations and the regional consultations provided input into the choice of subject matter for Sheffield and helped shape the discussions there. But most significant of all were the local studies which were held all across the world. Over 65,000 copies of the study guide were produced. The reports of local studies expressed a variety of viewpoints but through them all ran the theme that the new community of women and men is essential for the church. All of this material was carefully sifted and insights were shared with the participants at Sheffield. Unlike many consultations this was not a top-down operation but one in which the struggles and questions of many thousands of women and men were fed into the process. It was often slow and painful and the Sheffield study kept falling behind schedule but it marked a new era of local participation in a worldwide study.

By the time Connie Parvey recounted the story of the dream to the Africa Consultation in Ibadan in September of 1980, 200 written reports had been received, a great many of them from Europe and North America. Why? Connie asked the African participants. Did this mean that there was more interest there or that the study was a Western creation? And she explained the imbalance in communication resources of First and Third World churches. "From the rich countries, many of the reports are beautifully printed and prepared, some even with drawings and specially designed and with beautiful covers. All are typed on efficient electric typewriters. But from Africa and from some parts of Asia, we received reports handwritten on ordinary school paper. This gives us a clue to the problem: communication, or rather, the maldistribution of communication."

Communication in the West is easy, she said. One can simply telephone, direct dial almost anywhere at off hours, and it is not expensive. Copy and printing machines abound, travel is easy, networks are formed across national or regional boundaries. But in Africa, for example, it is quicker to send invitations to a conference in Ghana from Geneva than from East to West Africa. England was chosen for the international consultation because the cheapest, most frequent travel is in and out of London. Despite the maldistribution of resources, solid preparation for the conference was done in Third World regional consultations and local groups.

The consultations and local studies reflected the cultural context of the participants. Thailand was concerned about prostitution of the very poor. In India it was apparent that within all castes women are subordinate. "There is a chain of hierarchy working against community." In Latin America it was the macho mentality. In the Middle East the Orthodox view of women predominated. In both Eastern and Western Europe and in North America the concerns about women and work and new roles for both women and men predominated. The concern for ordination (which is more prevalent in North America and Europe) and the deeply felt discrimination in theology and church structures against women raised a question there about whether women could remain in strong patriarchal churches. Another U.S. concern was racism (the study there was mainly among white, middle-class persons).

What became apparent from the reports and the meetings was the same thing that emerged from the 1951 World Council study—that no matter what the church or where it was located there were men dominating at the top and many women serving at the bottom. And, as in the study three decades earlier, the opportunities for capable women in the society exceeded those in the church. This was true in Protestant, Roman Catholic, Anglican, and Orthodox churches. And the preoccupation was with greater empowerment for all the laity and a search for new methods of cooperation that would avoid the old male, competitive, authoritarian model. All across the world there was concern that Scripture had been used (or misused) to subject women in church, family, and society. The theological question of imaging God only in male, patriarchal terms emerged along with historical questions of the prominence of women saints and heroines.

The Meat and the Bones

There is an old African saying, "If you never ask for the meat, you will only get the bones." So Kowodo Ankrah, the acting general secretary of the All Africa Council of Churches, opened the Africa Regional Consultation. "African women are not asking enough," he said. At the Africa Consultation, organized by Isabella Johnston of the AACC office of Church, Family, and Society in cooperation with Mercy Oduyoye of the University of Ibadan and Daisy Obi, director of the Institute of Church and Society, where the consultation was held, it was apparent that women were hungry for meat.

In keeping with the spontaneity sought in this study, there were no presentations undertaken long in advance. Speakers were identified less than forty-eight hours in advance and the format of the meeting was to encourage frank exchange. Such African customs as polygamy, the role of traditional religion, and the political stance of women in some tribes and villages provided a backdrop to discussions of the present-day role of women in African church and society.

Most hotly debated at the African meeting were the issues of sexuality and celibacy. Some men argued that the church should not emphasize sexuality. "Sexuality is a mystery. If we talk about it, we will become just like the West where anything goes." But the women disagreed as they gave example after example of sexism in the church where women were not only excluded from power but treated as sex objects. The outcome was the call for a new theological/spiritual foundation and practice in partnership, sharing with both men and women being engaged in sex education for young girls and boys.

In India the area consultation expressed a belief that was echoed in many other places: everyone is first a human person and then a woman or man. "People should think of themselves in this order, as women are first persons and then women, men are first persons and then men, homosexuals are first persons and then homosexuals" (Bangalore, pp. 86–87). The group in India felt that except for biological differences, all other differences are culturally, socially, and economically determined. "Accepting the fact of biological differences, should men exploit and victimize women?" (Bangalore, p. 87).

Indians reported another observation that had global echoes: the subservient role of women has been determined by society, and women themselves have inculcated these attitudes and have been culturally conditioned to accept their role. This discovery occurred in Swiss villages and Canadian cities as well as in Asia, Latin America, and Africa. "Subservience has even been made a virtue," the Asian report said. "Women are excluded from a productive role in society. They are not paid for the work they do in their homes. The church supports the role society has assigned women and gives it religious sanction.''

Marriage and the nuclear family both reflect and perpetuate the exploitative nature of society at large, the Asian consultation agreed. ''Single women are not recognized as having a proper status in Indian society as everything centers around marriage for women.'' There was surprisingly little about single women in any of the reports. The Asian group made another discovery that was to turn out to be true in most of the world: the male-dominated media devalue woman and turn her into a commodity. The practice of dowry and prostitution as well as jobs like receptionist, nurse, and airline hostess can reduce women to commodities.

The family as training ground for conformity was highlighted in a speech by D. D. Pitamber at Bangalore. In this astringent view of the family, it is suggested that nothing will change in male-female relationships unless we begin with family. ''Jesus Christ felt that a family has an option to build itself either according to the values of the kingdom of this world or of the Kingdom of God. . . . In Matt. 10:34–37 we have the most radical and shocking statement by Jesus on this issue. He says, 'For I have come to set a man against his father, and a daughter against her mother, and a daughter-in-law against her mother-in-law.'

''I am sure that no minister can utter such words in his church without inviting the wrath of the people. He [note gender] will be immediately thrown out from the church. And yet these words of Jesus were aimed at the most important institution of the society. The words amount to inciting people against the traditional patterns of human relationships. Actually what Jesus is saying here is that those who would like to enter the Kingdom of God will have to challenge any relationship which is against the will of God. Any relationship which is based on the exploitation of one by another is against the will of God. Therefore, the structures of human relationships which contribute to the dehumanization of persons must be challenged and destroyed'' (Pitamber, Bangalore, p. 67).

Identity and Family

Listen to one European man's reflections:

There is a woman who is tired of acting weak when she knows she is strong, and there is a man who is tired of appearing strong when he feels vulnerable.

There is a woman who is tired of acting dumb, and there is a man who is burdened with the constant expectation of knowing everything.

There is a woman who is tired of being called "an emotional female," and there is a man who is denied the right to weep and to be gentle.

There is a woman who is called unfeminine when she competes and there is a man for whom competition is the only way to prove his masculinity.

There is a woman who is tired of being a sex object and there is a man who must worry about his potency.

There is a woman who feels "tied down" by her children and there is a man who is denied the full pleasure of shared parenthood.

There is a woman who is denied meaningful employment or equal pay, and there is a man who must bear full financial responsibility for another human being.

Bringing the promise of New Community,
there is a woman who takes a step toward her own
liberation, and there is a man who finds the way
to freedom is made a little easier.

In the family in the new community envisioned at Sheffield, the call to freedom and participation, as well as the call to devotion to family life, will be more equally shared by women and men. At Sheffield there were people from extended families with strong traditional structures and people from nuclear families with fluid structures. Both styles of family life were marked by change and weakening of the basic family groups and patterns inherited from the past.

"The oppressor in the church, society, and home is the

same," according to the section on Marriage, Family, and Life Styles at Sheffield. What did this startling statement mean? Blame it on Adam? Actually they were saying that the kinds of relationships, roles, and attitudes which persons have within church and society carry over into the family and vice versa. The kinds of relationships in home and family, including attitudes and behavior, are reflected in everyday encounters in church and society. All three realities shape and reinforce socialization of women and men with damage to both.

Abandoning the term "alternate life style" because it seemed to imply deviant or less complete life styles than those chosen by the majority, the section gave serious attention to changing patterns of family life. They discovered that there is no appropriate term for familial relationships not marked by legal or blood ties. The Sheffield section report said:

> We are concerned about finding ways to work together as a community of Women and Men in the Church on issues which affect the total community. We note that in most areas of the world, many people now live in nuclear families, but there are other family types which are also part of a total community: single people, lone partners, homosexuals, separated, divorced, and re-married persons, persons married outside of the Church, persons living in community life, etc. . . . In a time when we call on the Church to support families in the face of enormous societal pressures, the Church must give support to new realities and changing patterns of familial life.

The report regarding family life and changing families highlights the need of the church to give more attention and support not only to the causes of family disorganization but to support families in changing situations, giving special attention to the nurture and development of children and to a broader context of community and church that encourages extended families in various forms in differing cultural situations.

Human Being

Human being . . .
Why are man and woman created in God's creation?
For the sake of being opposition and comparison?
Or being an enemy to one and other?
Or being a manipulating-exploiting tool for one and other?
Human being . . .
Woman-man exists for the truth of agape-living
Man-woman exists for the truth of power-uniting
Woman-man exists for the truth of being whole
Man-woman exists for the truth of being one.
Human being . . .
To be man and woman is to be supportive to one and other
Not for being enemies but cosustainers
Not for despising but for praising
Not for selling-buying but for living in dignity.
Human being . . .
Thou art mono and not duo
Thou art made cosustainer and not solo
That's the truth of being
Human being.

Maen Pongudom
Thailand

3

Becoming Human
in the New Community

Elisabeth and Jürgen Moltmann, in a dialogue presentation on the first full day at Sheffield, set the stage for an examination of patriarchal religion and demonstrated ways this concept had warped not only women but also men. Jürgen, a well-known theologian of hope, was familiar to many through his writings. To most non-Europeans, Elisabeth Moltmann-Wendel was new. The wife-husband team shared with us their common discoveries as they sought the new community.

Elisabeth began (though Jürgen was later to say that chivalry was one of the things men need to give up) by claiming that church history begins when a few women set out to pay their respects to their dead friend Jesus. "It begins when contrary to all reasons and hope, a few women identify themselves and do what *they* consider to be right, what in their eyes equals equality of life, namely, loving one who sacrificed his life, never abandoning him as dead. Church history begins when Jesus comes to them, greets them, lets them touch him just as he had touched and restored them in their lives. Church history begins when the women are told to share this experience, this life they now comprehend, which their hands have handled, with the men."

But Elisabeth quickly noted that this Matthew account of the Easter appearance has never been known as the beginning of church history. Instead it begins officially with the men apostles and "officially, no women are present on that occasion." Right down to the present time, she noted, many churches trace their origins back to this apostolic succession. "Almost all the leaders of these churches are male and depend mostly on males for their order and ideas. The idea of God is conceived mainly in masculine terms; male leadership roles are used to describe what God does—he reigns, judges, governs; God corresponds to what men would like to be—judge, king, ruler, army commander." In the process, she said, women's experiences of Jesus have been forgotten—the Jesus who is friend, who shares their lives, offers warmth and tenderness in their loneliness and power-lessness. "The feminist movement in the Western world has given many women the courage to discover themselves, to express again their own religious experiences, to read the Bible with fresh eyes and to rediscover their original and distinctive role in the gospel."

Anticipating the arguments that were to come in Sheffield, she said that for such women feminism is "not a white Western bourgeois movement but one deeply rooted in the gospel." Nor did she blame men for the patriarchate. "Men should not feel or be held personally responsible for it. The patriarchate is a cultural form dating back thousands of years . . . but in the last two centuries in particular it has produced disastrous alliances with colonialism and racism, capitalism and sexism, which have led us to start seeking the fundamental causes of these evils."

Is God on the side of the patriarchate? When his time came, Jürgen argued that it was not Christianity that in-troduced the patriarchate into the world. But Christianity proved inadequate to opposing the ancient and widespread system of male domination and soon found itself taken over by men and serving the system. Leaving the male Lord God behind, "we shall discover from the sources of Christian-ity the sociable God, the God who can suffer, the uniting God, the God of fellowship and community." And in dis-covering this living God, man too will be delivered from the distortions of suppression, what instincts he had to con-trol, what roles he was taught to adopt. "He was trained to be a worker, a soldier, father of the family, breadwinner, a conqueror, and ruler. He was ruled by the anxiety to not be a mere cipher and by the need to make something of himself. . . ."

Far from benefiting from the patriarchate in his emotional life, the man is cut in half, Jürgen argued. "It split him into a subject consisting of reason and will, an object of the heart, feelings, and physical needs." Another product of the pa-triarchate is the division of woman into mother and wife. "Unresolved mother fixations and machismo against other women go together. There must be an end to both mothering and domination if the man is to become free and adult."

He painted a chilling portrait of the lonely majesty of the God of the patriarchate, all powerful, incapable of being influenced or of suffering. Between this heavenly Father and the mystery of Jesus' Abba-Father, Jürgen asserted there is no connection at all. To counter this Lord God defined only by his function as ruler and proprietor of the world, he issued a challenge to men to discover the living God and life for themselves and then in community with women, shaking off their nightmare and pressures of the patriarchate. "What happens to us here is rather like what happened to the disciples who hear the women's Easter message and then half believing, half disbelieving, go off to find for themselves the Living Lord who they had forsaken shortly before the crucifixion."

Women, Elisabeth believes, should lead in this way to a new community of women and men. And she bombards Jürgen with a series of questions: Can the Christian tradition offer us any help to extricate ourselves from this life? Where do the sources and motivations exist for this in respect to our identity? What Christian traditions can support us on the way to wholeness? What Christian traditions can also help the man to be whole and give him an identity other than that of a patriarch?

While admitting that biblical, Christian, and church traditions were mainly written and edited by dominating men, he says that the history of the defeated is present in the victor's stories. He suggests that the first account of creation in the priestly tradition has been almost completely forgotten in the second account which stresses Eve's guilt.

Jürgen speaks of the ancient but suppressed tradition of the maternal office of the Holy Spirit. And he sees the doctrine of the Trinity ("undoubtedly difficult and abstract") as paving the way for the story of the masculine Lord God. Speaking personally, he said that he was helped by the thought that the mighty man may be an imitation of the Almighty but only a human community in which human beings have all things in common and share all things, irrespective of individual characteristics, can be an image of the triune God. "This thought helped me to seek God not only in heaven above, not only in the inward depths of the soul, but also and above all between us in our community."

As to our traditions, the German theologian of hope came

through once again with an emphasis on hope. While acknowledging the value of traditions, he said, "No tradition can settle the future. At best traditions can only prepare the way into the future. What the Spirit itself creates is always something new and full of surprises. . . . Christianity is more than a tradition, it is hope." Not all members of the conference agreed with Jürgen on the casting of the Holy Spirit as female or maternal or in the role ascribed to the patriarchate. In particular, some Orthodox participants held a much more benevolent view of the patriarchate and allowed a stronger, more active role for tradition.

Elisabeth spoke candidly about some women who can pray "Our Father-Mother in Heaven . . . ." "Feminist theology—its very name sends cold shivers up the spines of many theologians—is the only way they can speak freely and discover themselves to be daughters of God. Women have a culture of their own. It is very different in the different countries of Asia and Africa. It is a more concrete and pictorial culture than the corresponding male culture though it is often buried underground. For us, therefore, theo-fantasy takes its place alongside theology and frequently excavates the buried sources." Theo-fantasy, she said, takes not only past experiences and traditions into account but also contemporary and coming experiences. Claiming that life is more diverse and colorful than any written tradition, she engaged in the theo-fantasy of her own: men sitting at the feet of women listening, as Mary sat at the feet of Jesus.

A note that was struck many times in the conference appeared here: women do not wish to become like men, exercising power insensitively and giving up their uniqueness. "A new community can only mature and bear fruit if women remain autonomous human beings, retaining their singularity, specificity, distinctiveness as women. In the church we are used to thinking of the church as a "great big loving family in which everyone is self-effacing for the sake of others, forgetful of self in the interest of a great cause. Everyone and everything should be united in one great first person plural." But if women and men are to come together in a new community, they must bid goodbye to such wishful thinking, Elisabeth warned. Each must separately accept the pain of division "and even the possible deprivation of love.'' A hard reeducation is ahead for men, Jürgen believes.

But what about the churches? Elisabeth resumes her role of interrogator. ''Can they cope with women coming of age? Is the church prepared to take them seriously?'' In answering this question, Jürgen makes a revolutionary suggestion. Referring to the church's preoccupation with service, care, sacrifice for others, and responsibility as ''this dictatorship of love, this patriarchate of love,'' he suggests that a Christian ''always on active service and existing for others'' might actually be practicing a kind of concealed domination.

At the end of their dialogue they returned to Elisabeth's starting point of church history: the women at the tomb. She questioned: Is it possible to begin trusting the Holy Spirit once again? ''The spirit of extremists, crackpots, outsiders, visionaries, the spirit of those who saw and touched life as did the women on Easter morning and whose reports seemed to the disciples no more than idle tales? Can the age-old distrust of women except when they speak cautiously, rationally, and in male language be dispelled?''

Jürgen answers honestly: ''Many find it hard to accept the feminist appeal to the Holy Spirit because they are not sure whether it is really the Holy Spirit or some other spirit they are appealing to.'' And he comes back to the story they began with and asks how the women actually recognized the living Christ. They recognized him not as ghost or someone else because they had remained faithful to him right up to the death on the cross. ''They recognized him at once by the marks of the nails and by the way of dealing with them, familiar to them from experience. Nor is the life-giving spirit to be recognized in any other way.''

But why did it happen that the experience of these women ''sank without a trace,'' Elisabeth wonders. Why didn't a viable community of women and men emerge 2,000 years ago? And she wonders if it was the fault of the women who showed more confidence in the social structure than in themselves . . . who obeyed men more than God, who retired to their ancient female roles and failed to trust the power of the resurrection. . . . And she ends on a note of hope: we must all trust ourselves and trust our capacity to communicate life by all our senses and capacities.

And she calls us all—women and men—not to capitulate in the face of invincible structures and never to lapse back again, in body, soul, and spirit so that this spark may spread to men, brothers, fathers, mothers, and children.

Breaking the Ice: Tradition

The dynamic of faith, hope, and love. It began at Pentecost and even before that with the encounter of a few women with the risen Christ on Easter morning. From there it has swept like a wave through the world and the centuries. A conveyor of energy; a ferment unceasingly rising and activating the dough of the institutions. It is the place of an ever-renewed event, a place where each of us in the fellowship of all—the communion of saints—can meet the Lord of the church in an ever-renewed way.

So Elisabeth Behr-Sigel, a Russian Orthodox theologian from Paris, described Tradition. Speaking on the Orthodox tradition as resource for the renewal of women and men in community, Dr. Behr-Sigel told the Sheffield consultation that faithfulness to tradition does not mean a kind of sacralization of the past, of the history of the church. "Tradition is not a kind of immutable monster, a prison in which we would be confined forever. It is a stream of life, driven and impregnated by the energies of the Holy Spirit, a steam which unavoidably carries historical and, therefore, transitory elements and even ashes and cinders. Sometimes it seems to stand still as if imprisoned in a layer of ice, but under the rigid frozen surface, there run the clear waters of spring. It is our task, with the help of God's mercy, to break through the ice, especially the ice in our slumbering, frozen hearts."

In a profound, poetic address the Orthodox woman shared the riches of her ancient tradition as the consultation sought for the new community in a way radically different from other approaches of the consultation. This address set before the group the mystical vision expressed in icons, lovingly and beautifully described by the speaker, as a source of inspiration for the daily struggle for the real community of men and women.

Dr. Elisabeth Behr-Sigel described an icon that is traditionally seen in Orthodox churches above the "royal doors." Together with the Trinity, it represents one of the major expressions of Orthodox spirituality, she told us. "In the center there is Christ in majesty. Converging toward him and heading a procession of men and women who represent the saints of all ages, there are, on one side, John the Baptist and, on the other, the praying Virgin, the *Theotokos*. Both processions move toward Christ as fulfillment, the fulfillment of humanity in God, in which neither male nor female is denied—in which the opposition is overcome by their conversion to the Lord in their mutual relationship as well as their individual personalities.

"Psychology, sociology, psychoanalysis, and Marxist analysis are human sciences to be used with discernment," she said. These interpretive sciences can enable us to disclose, up to a certain extent, "the mechanism of the behavior of the fallen Adam, the determinisms that hang heavily on humanity and are entangled with its anxieties, its egotism, its contradictory desires. Real faith in God, the one who is altogether other, and the Good News, the radical newness that he proclaims to humankind, need not fear these sciences." But they alone, when not accompanied by deep change (*metanoia*), cannot create a new future. "They prove unable to haul man out of the cave in which (according to Plato's profound myth) he is shackled facing the wall. Strength of overcoming is given to the believer who in faith freely clings to the Word of God and the vision granted the church."

The "celestial vision" can prevent our struggles from getting diluted by utopian humanism or sinking into the "moving sands of violence." But she warned that the celestial vision is inspiration for, not a solution to, specific problems set by specific situations. It must inspire action. "The Western temptation is to ignore the vision while the temptation of the Orthodox is to dodge the effort necessary to translate it to the present situation."

Dr. Behr-Sigel had a good and different word to say for the patriarchal society, even for St. Paul. Noting how the historical church has been condemned for its patriarchal model, she suggested closer definition. Admitting that this so-called model had influenced the institutional structure of the church and marked its "mentalities," she said the church is historical reality in this world and therefore has not escaped this influence. But the patriarchal model is not "wholly negative in its ideal view of the family and society. It does not necessarily imply lack of respect toward women. Within its structure and through a language which seems to remain patriarchal, the church has brought a radically new message."

While St. Paul is accused of having exhorted the wife to submit to her husband, we tend to ignore the context of loving kindness and service, she observed. The passage opens with the words: "Be subject to one another out of reverence for Christ" (Eph. 5:21). "In the same way, Paul's preaching lifts the union of man and woman, even in its fleshly aspect, to the dignity of a sign of the mysterious love of Christ and the Church—of supreme love, a love so deep that one gives himself or herself to the other—a love in which there is no room for dominator or dominated."

The ferment of the gospel shatters old, outdated, and oppressive structures, Dr. Behr-Sigel affirmed. "I recognize the genius of the tradition of the church in the women's movement which claims that women are to be respected as free and responsible persons. It is in the dynamic of the authentic tradition (and not in ephemeral ideologies) that we find the source of eternal, the source of our real liberation." In the life of the energizing force of this tradition, she said, "We are called to invent new styles of communal life, new styles of family life in our society and church."

Professor Nicholas Lossky spoke on the role of liturgy and iconography in the Orthodox tradition at the Faith and Order Commission in Lima, Peru, in January 1982. The one figure who occupies a central place in relation to Christ in Orthodox iconography is the Virgin Mary, a woman. He said, "We venerate her not only because of her womb—she bore the son of God and is therefore the Mother of God (*Theotokos*)—but also because she, above all other creatures, heard the word of God and kept it (Luke 11:27–28). She is the very type of holiness in the church where there is 'neither male nor female.' And yet, though there is neither male nor female, in this liturgical iconographic experience of the Orthodox church, here is a woman who remains a woman, the Mother of God." To Professor Lossky, this suggests that the true meaning of "neither male nor female" is not to be sought in a kind of neutrality, of "false equality, or sexlessness or abolition of all differences. The specificity is maintained, there is no loss of maleness or femaleness; men are still men, women are still women in the church and the new order of the kingdom. It is the relationship, the type of partnership, that changes. The relationship is one in which human beings are no longer defined merely by their biological role or type. The relations are no longer ruled by acquisition, domination, servility. The relations are trans-figured, reconciled."

4

From Pyramid to Circle

What if the model for authority and community no longer were the pyramid of the hierarchy but the circle or perhaps the rainbow of colors, symbol of hope?

"Authority-in-Community," a paper prepared by a study group of the Commission on Faith and Order of the National Council of Churches, USA, chaired by Roman Catholic theologian Dr. Madeline Boucher, puts the issue succinctly. The presupposition of many is that authority is power, power is masculine, and powerlessness is feminine.

"On one side we have authority, power, the male: God as Father, Jesus Christ as Lord, and the pastor and father as representative of God and Christ. On the other side we have submission, powerlessness, the female—and no corresponding connection between God, Christ, and woman. In this view, power is understood as influence or control over others, and authority as the ability to wield such power," the report asserted.

Luther noted that "men have broad shoulders and narrow hips, and accordingly, they possess intelligence." The archbishop of Canterbury said in his opening address to the Sheffield Consultation, "Women, Luther asserted, ought to stay home; the way they were created indicates this for they have broad hips and a wide fundament to sit upon, keep house, bear and raise children." The head of the Anglican communion reminded us that Calvin had little better to say. He took the care of baptism from the midwives saying they should not usurp the function of men, "let alone the priests," by baptizing, and saw "the area of activity of women solely in terms of seducing or, if virtuous, child-rearing."

As the spiritual leader of a worldwide communion of millions, the remarks of the archbishop of Canterbury were of special interest to those present who believe that women should be ordained. In some parts of the Anglican communion, notably in North America, Africa, and Asia, women have entered the priesthood. But in England the priesthood is still denied them. Bishops and laity have voted in favor but priests of the Church of England have rejected sharing the ministry with women. The Most Reverend Robert Runcie, the present archbishop, has said that he sees no theological objection to ordination of women, but feels it would jeopardize his church's relationships with Rome and Constantinople. The Roman Catholic and Orthodox churches are resolutely against the ordination of women to the priesthood.

Observing that part of the heritage of Calvin and Luther is the fact that ministry is a masculine status organization, he argued that the contemplative nun, the nurse, the teacher, and social worker are "ministers" and some of them by definition feminine ministers. Overconcentration on the issues involved in the ordination of women, he said, may reinforce a clericalist view of the church that the only ministry worth exercising is an *ordained* one.

"Yet in my own communion and in the history of Western Christendom, Dame Julian of Norwich, Evelyn Underhill, and a whole host of persons who act as such diverse things as marriage guidance counselors and spiritual advisors without that being positively on their passports (though it would show in their diaries), in reality are ministers." Women who "do not necessarily see themselves as candidates for the priesthood do not see their contribution to the church solely in terms of altar flowers, inspiring as these creations may be." The archbishop offered a variety of roles of ministry for which he did not see ordination as necessary for women. They include medical work, counseling "the battered or hard pressed with their problems of pain or prayer," prisoners, prostitutes, homosexuals. Ascribing to women particular sensitivity to spirituality, the archbishop mentioned special courses which trained women "in recognition of their own selves, body, mind and spirits, wombs and wit."

The intrepid archbishop, having suggested a biological division of labor based on sexually ascribed charisma, reflected on the phenomenon called feminism. "The women's movement today is no longer simply feminist. It is not a united movement, and it is all the better for that. It divides between those who want to burn their bras, refuse to marry, and insist on doing all that men do—even to playing games which are anatomically painful, and those who ask for something more difficult to articulate. That something is the freedom to be women. It consists in *not* being constrained by male attitudes to the ministry, to the work, to the family, or above all to God." And Dr. Runcie found this uniqueness in the very depth of their being: in love for children, outreach beyond conventional boundaries, acceptance of a "measure of physical weakness, and this may breed not militancy but a very real humility." Above all, he said, women need to accept from others an understanding "that they just may not be simple shoulders and hips as Luther would have them, but more complex beings, perhaps even more complex than men, and for that reason may be a source of fear."

Dr. Runcie found the real message of the Christian feminist movement to be about "complementarity in ministry" and "the unity of sexes in the Godhead," and appealed to the insights of various traditions to dignify and legitimate differences and variations of ministry which men and women can bring to the unity of the church. If nothing else, the address validated his claim that there are a variety of opinions among women. Both men and women from churches that ordain women in addition to some Roman Catholics and Anglicans tended to feel that he was once again ascribing only certain functions to women without any discussion of whether they are equipped to exercise other functions. By appearing to exalt certain sensitive, helping ministries and spiritual disciplines as particularly appropriate to women, he seemed to say that these were not appropriate to men. To others at the consultation, notably Orthodox women, he stressed those values of superiority in service and spirituality which they believe to be at the heart of women's ministry and indeed of the patriarchate as well. News media inclined to see the archbishop's address as one which saw that ministry was to be shared.

Yet in one sense, the archbishop's appeal to see powerlessness transformed into a gift both for women themselves and others is an insight that many would agree upon. The North American paper on Authority-in-Community indicates that a new view of power might provide a fresh perspective and new, alternative ways of viewing power which may be closer than the old ways to the biblical way. The North American paper argues for something more than a redistribution of roles—"who will be powered and who the powerless"—and suggests an inclusive concept of authority-in-community.

What was troubling to many in Dr. Runcie's analysis was pointed out three decades earlier by Kathleen Bliss in her pioneering study on *The Service and Status of Women in the Churches:* "The nearer a service of women approaches to the ministerial functions, the more on edge the churches are about it." Dr. Bliss noted that women have traditionally exercised the functions of helping, serving, teaching, nursing, and supporting, but she found that even when women had proven themselves able to exercise other functions, such as preaching and administering the sacraments during times of war or emergency when men were unavailable, "an effort is always made at the time or afterwards either to abolish the form of service accepted in an emergency or justify and regularize it by an appeal to Scripture and to church tradition" (Bliss, p. 79).

Nearly all the churches say, in effect, "Women may serve in these ways, and will be called deaconesses or lay workers or directors of religious education, and in exceptional circumstances, they may do this or this with authority from such and such." The question of women in the ministry raises all the other questions on which churches differ, she said: the authority of the Bible and the criteria for its interpretation for modern needs, the nature of the ministry, the relationship of ministry and laity, and "the age-old question of the relationship of religion and sex which still exercises a powerful influence largely inexpressible in words."

In her study Dr. Bliss summarized the arguments for and against ordination of women in a variety of churches. At that time the modern debate was about thirty years old and, as she said, the question did not even come up in the Roman Catholic and Orthodox churches. She summarized their position: "There is scope for women in social work of the churches and in education and if their calling is to prayer, they are in convents." Thirty years ago it would have been hard to imagine that the head of religious women in the Roman Catholic Church in North America would be so bold as to bring the matter of the ordination of women before Pope John Paul as did Sister Theresa Kane.

The survey of the World Council of Churches published in 1952 revealed that in the free churches of North America and Britain (Methodist, Presbyterian, Congregationalist, Baptist) women were being admitted to the pastoral ministry but their role was hardly that of men and getting appointments to larger churches was almost impossible. While a Chinese bishop in the Anglican Church in China who had appointed a woman to the position of priest raised the question in that communion, it would be a quarter of a century before the Anglican churches began to do so. The state Lutheran churches in Scandinavia had a number of theologically trained women and in Norway there was a law against barring the ministry to women. In Germany and Austria during the war, the theologically trained *vikarean,* a kind of pastoral assistant, had served in many places where men were no longer available, even to preaching and administering the sacraments. Churches in Asia, Africa, and Latin America followed the traditions of their "parent" bodies. In Argentina and a few other places, seminaries were beginning to give theological training to young women. But full women ministers were a rarity and existed mostly in North America.

It was not until 1980 that the United Methodist Church in the USA elected its first woman bishop, Bishop Marjorie Matthews, although women had been ordained since 1956. In recent years the Episcopal Church in the USA, the Anglican churches in Canada, New Zealand, and elsewhere have ordained women. But the Roman Catholic church, the Orthodox churches, and most Anglican churches, containing the majority of the world's Christians, continue to reserve the priesthood for men. The community study calls for a fresh look at the ordination and at what it means to be clergy and laity.

The Priesthood of All Believers

Fundraisers, cooks, cleaners, decorators, educators, and secretaries: cheap and unpaid labor. The Sheffield section dealing with ministry and worship in the new community found that in some parts of the world lay women are the majority of membership in churches but hold few positions of responsibility in their governing bodies. Both laymen and women are restricted in their theological development by lack of training and placement opportunities.

Ordained women at the consultation felt the issue of women in the ordained priesthood had been sidestepped. The section dealing with the ordained ministry prefaced its statement within "the unique ecumenical context" of the World Council of Churches. "We are aware of the complexity and diversity of existing situations within and between the different churches. The state of the discussion is also at different stages in different cultures. Amongst the churches there is a plurality of practices embracing those who do ordain women, those who do not, and those who are hesitant for ecumenical reasons," the ministry section explained.

Sheffield acknowledged that the issues involved in ordination touch us at our deepest level, "embodied as they are in liturgy, symbolism, and spirituality." No real progress can be made if the issue is forced without a total awareness of what is involved, the section report said. But a call for more sociological and theological investigation was not enough for a number of ordained women present. They looked for a more explicit statement. Women of the Orthodox tradition present felt quite differently. If the report was too weak for some, it was too strong for others. There were a dozen or so Roman Catholic women present fully participating in the consultation. The difficulty of forging an ecumenical consensus on an issue which has divided the church for centuries became acutely apparent here.

A young American woman, Katherine Johnson Lieurance, spoke to the pain of ordained women concerning the issue. Noting that the report on tradition had commented that his maleness was not significant to Christ's reconciling ministry, the American woman said that many felt that they would fail their responsibility if they did not express solidarity with those women who long for ordination and with those now ordained who face problems of assignment and placement.

"Many of us here from the industrial nations and developing countries, men and women, support the manifold ministries of women in the church—one of which is the ordained ministry," she said. The report presented has spoken "to the traditions of the church, explaining that the maleness of Jesus was not significant to his reconciling ministry. I want to underline and strengthen this point, knowing that the ordination of women is not *the* issue at this consultation but it is *an* issue."

Dr. Madeline Boucher, the Fordham University theologian and Roman Catholic, referred to the archbishop of Canterbury's reluctance to endorse the ordination of women because of relationships with Roman Catholic and Orthodox churches as a cop-out (National Catholic News Service, July 20, 1981, Report by Jo-Ann Price Baehr). Boucher told NCNS that the ecumenical unity view against ordination is a cop-out to keep women oppressed in the church. "As long as the church excludes women from its symbolic center, you can't speak of true equality. And if there is no true equality, there is no true unity," she asserted.

At the worship service on the final evening of the Sheffield Consultation when women and men shared experiences in many forms, Margaret Davies summed up the feelings of those women who felt called to the priesthood and were denied it by their church in a poem called "Dear Mother Church."

Dear Mother Church

Dear Mother Church,

    I cannot call you Mother
    Rather you were the
godmother, present at my
baptism, and at the christening party—
    the wicked godmother who
brought me your gifts.

    You brought me a tablet of
stone bearing its petrifying
command to sacrifice myself
at all times "for the sake of
The Church."

    You brought me the gift
of a tape-recorder so that
conscience could repeat your
demands.

    You brought me the gift
of chains of guilt to
bind me to yourself should I
erase the tapes.

    Then you bade me sacrifice
myself on the altar of the
Church's service, but you
refused to let me stand at
the Altar to serve others
with the bread of life, until I was too old.

Dear Mother Church,

At Sheffield I have risen
from the ashes of conscience
into the freedom of the spirit
of love.

Dear Mother Church,

May I offer you a gift?
The gift of a heart-transplant.

Margaret Davies
Great Britain

5

A Home for Humanity

Psychiatrist Jean Baker Miller took as her topic at Sheffield the sense of self in women and men in relationship to critical world questions. Admitting that hers was a Western cultural bias, she outlined four issues that plague contemporary Western "man": lack of a convincing high purpose and an interest beyond self-interest; inability to find a sense of community and even communication; failure to organize knowledge and technology for the benefit of human beings and the inability to "encompass the development of others"; and acting on the basis of belief that one's interest is synonymous with the interest of others.

Discussing power and powerlessness from another vantage point, the American doctor painted a picture of women as psychologically more prone to admit to feelings of vulnerability concerning emotions and to admit weaknesses because of cultural conditioning, and men as more guarded concerning emotions (or more likely to display the emotion of anger rather than to admit weakness). According to her analysis, only by recognizing feelings of weakness and knowing that they are not shameful can one move from them. "The coerced flight from vulnerability forecloses large parts of growth and consciousness for men. Women, both superficially and deeply, are more closely in touch with the experience of living . . . that is to say, in touch with reality."

Since men consider feelings "unmanly," this reinforces the humiliation of men about such experiences and encourages the attack on women who have been made to embody weakness. Removing feelings from the realm of the acceptable keeps the total society from admitting the danger and doubt we grow up with and from finding a way out. "Women, meanwhile, have provided all sorts of personal and social supports which help to keep men going. These props keep men, and therefore the total culture, able to sustain its mythology and refusal to admit the need for better arrangements for all. Everyone loses in the end but this loss is kept obscure." Dr. Miller acutely remarks that while women are seen to be "more emotional," there is "no such thing as more emotional." Every thought and action, she argues, is simultaneously emotion and action. "What is probably true is that women have been attuned to the emotional aspects which are present in every event. Male culture has emphasized rationality, so-called problem solving, analytical thinking and the like. The emotions have not been seen as an aid in this pursuit, but rather as an impediment, often close to evil." And she argues that being touched with the emotions is not an impediment to intellectual or analytical thinking but can enhance the process.

In looking back at Kathleen Bliss's report, it is interesting to see how this very intelligent woman faulted women for being largely uninterested in theology. She found less to blame in what she considered their lack of organizational leadership. "Women have never been the makers of institutions: they are often accused of not being able to think in terms of rules, procedures, organization, and logical deduction. That is true, and it has been a weakness in women" (Bliss, p. 200). Bliss balances this by saying that perhaps organizations in the modern world have become a burden to us and occupy too large a space. Both Bliss and Jean Baker Miller are ultimately arguing for a new relationship between the sexes. Armed with insights from Margaret Mead's *Male and Female* and the then recently published Simone de Beauvoir's *The Second Sex,* Dr. Bliss says one thing revealed by the report from the churches around the world was that theoretical argument about what woman can, may, or ought to do is useless. "Such arguments quickly lead into the quagmire of discussing what woman is, as though they were given a finalized collection of attributes and limitations." In her summary pages, Dr. Bliss argues that her long experience as the homemaker, the one who brings forth and cares for young life, "makes the woman the one of the human partnership most capable of turning into something of a home for humanity the society which man has created and depersonalized by his techniques. To do this, in the largest sense, is 'church work'" (Bliss, p. 201).

Dr. Bliss was pleading for greater recognition for the

kinds of welfare work many women engaged in, and for this work to be considered ministry, "ministry the Church does not yet recognize or assist the women to fulfill." She ended her book with a quote from a woman in Berlin who said that the World Council's questions about the role of women in the churches were interesting but the most important question had not been asked at all. The life of the church, according to this woman, is no longer carried out in its organizations but where people are: in houses and factories and offices, where Christians meet with others. "So the first question should be, what does the church mean in the lives of women? What chance does the church give to women to be its presence at home and in their work?"

Jean Baker Miller, in the 1980s, looks at some of the same questions and also finds that women may be able to make more of a home for humanity but seeks that ability for men as well. She would probably agree with the archbishop of Canterbury that women have been encouraged to be involved with emotional and personal relationships.

The point is that these relationships are important for men too, but men have not been able to encompass this as primary concern. As a psychotherapist, Dr. Miller sees trouble coming from the distortions that both sexes have been taught, and trouble for women because of "the belief that full satisfaction should come only from relationships and often only from relationships at any price."

What Runcie sees as women's special sensitivity for interpersonal ministries, Bliss sees as home building for humanity and Miller calls fostering the development of other people. But Miller points out that fallacy of a culture that says "men will do the important work: women will tend to the lesser task of helping human beings to develop." She says the fostering and enhancing of another person's development have been minimized even by terms such as nurturing and caretaking. This sense of playing a part in helping the development of others as an essential part of one's identity is not encouraged in men as "an inner and thorough requirement of their sense of what it is to exist, to be a person."

"This requirement has not been made of the male sex, which controls the operation and the thinking of our institutions and therefore controls all of us," Dr. Miller warned.

Stressing that she was not arguing that women were more virtuous or saintly, or that they were biologically conditioned to relate, or that they should remain in their secondary places, she outlined a vision of mutuality, cooperation, and creativity in which women are joined by men and children to find their way out of the dilemma.

The questions of complementarity, a vision of mutuality, of dualism, of identity, and relationships of women and men were addressed in one of the preliminary consultations, the Niederaltaich Consultation "Towards a Theology of Human Wholeness." Held at an abbey in the Bavarian countryside in the Federal Republic of Germany, this consultation brought eighteen participants together, among them a theologian, a physicist, a medical doctor, and a psychiatrist. Here Protestants were in the minority with three Orthodox and eight Roman Catholics present. The abbey has a long commitment to Christian unity with some living according to the Byzantine rite while others continue to live in the tradition of St. Benedict. Once again North Americans and Europeans outnumbered those from developing nations. The experiential approach to the subject included case studies from various countries. From Latin America, Julia Campos presented a harsh picture of the role of women there.

"Women have been the most direct victims of injustices. The lack of a real sense of identity begins at birth when the fact of being born female already implies rejection and inferiority. A female is considered as an object that can be fondled—first by her parents and then, as a young wife, by her husband. As an adult woman she often sees no other meaning for her life than hard work. She frequently lacks real affection and may thus live without hope. The daily experience of isolated suffering hardens her personality and is accepted by her as fate. Everything, being the will of God, is going to remain as it is. This attitude is especially prevalent in the lower classes where the oppression of the socioeconomic structures is felt most intensely" (Niederaltaich Report, p.13).

The presence of the churches, both Protestant and Roman Catholic, according to Ms. Campos, has done little to alleviate the oppression of women. In many places, she says, the Good News about freedom recorded in Luke has not been announced. The gospel as the dynamic for a new being has not been presented in such a way that it can positively affect the life of all women, men, and children. Further, the moralistic way the gospel has been presented only in terms of individual good and evil with heavy moralistic emphasis and omission of concern for justice and injustice has kept women from seeing who they are or what their condition is.

Dr. Maen Pongudom of Thailand told the participants that in his country the desire to escape from poverty (coupled with ignorance) had led thousands of the girls from the country to be massage parlor prostitutes. Modernization in Thailand means a place of international bed affairs. "When you look through the glass walls of the massage parlors, you do not see the beautiful *imago dei*, but dehumanized creatures with numbers and prices. The *imago dei* is without numbers and it is priceless" (Niederaltaich Report, p. 14).

From Zaire came an examination of Kongo society which revealed that despite polygamy, dowry, demand for bridal virginity, and the double standard of sexual morality, the female child within the home is not inferior to the male. The clan revolves around her to a certain extent. Neither man nor woman is tied to the other but only to the clan. "Furthermore, traditional Kongo culture does not impose any sexist language. Each is a *muntu* (person), all possess the same vital strength which helps them to become *nganga* (priest, medium, healer) and *knulu* (ancestor) according to their qualities and virtues."

Western missionary churches and the colonial administration had a patriarchal character that altered these positive elements of the traditional relationships between women and men. Today the church has Sunday school leaders and consecrated parish pastors, founders and spiritual leaders of ecclesial communities, but the church structures are still "too much influenced by the traditional tendencies of male domination and Western, patriarchal biblical teaching."

"Matriarchy has been characteristic, at least within the clan, of Kongo society and of several other African cultures," and the African woman suggested that "the pattern of matriarchal society is often reflected in the African independent churches along with the rich area for revitalized images of God and new forms of human community" (Niederaltaich Report, p. 19).

Rose Zoé-Obianga, professor at the University of Nigeria, helped the Sheffield consultation discover some resources in African tradition that might help in the renewal of the church. As one of the plenary speakers, Rose was one of two to give a major address in a language other than English. She spoke in French, not an indigenous but a colonial language, and non-French speakers were assisted by both a written translation and simultaneous interpretation. English has been called the Latin of the ecumenical movement, and there has been serious attention paid in recent years to the cultural problem involved in this monolinguism. The truth is that most mother tongue English speakers do not have another language while most Third World Christians never have the opportunity to speak their own languages but always have to speak a European language, usually that of their former colonizers. This gives the person whose education has been English a decided edge over others. Officially the World Council's languages were French, English, and German, reflecting its North American/European origins. In recent years Spanish has been added, which has greatly helped in providing participation from Latin Americans. Without the work of translators, interpreters, and the new lightweight translation equipment, the ecumenical movement could never have advanced as it has. But with all the expense and expertise involved, there is still a terrible burden on those who must always communicate outside their accustomed linguistic thought forms.

I Am Because I Participate

Beginning with the assertion that we live in a time when the traditional models organizing community life of Christians are "fetters of freedom," Zoé-Obianga said this is obvious in the failure of the "normal and harmonious integration of women" into the decision-making bodies of the church and in respect to the demystification of structures and domination inherent in them. Frustrated women find themselves limited to secondary roles in the church, their status often being higher in the surrounding communities.

Rediscovering the African heritage is no easy task, for both the colonizers and the missionaries were destroyers of African culture and tradition. The tragedy, Zoé-Obianga finds, is that the first-generation Christian elites were completely alienated. To become Christians they contributed to the complete destruction of their African cultural personality, often unwittingly. "For them to follow Jesus meant completely abandoning one's own [culture] and putting on another. If we are to link up again with tradition, we have to do so only with the scraps of all that constituted our originality."

Calling language the supreme instrument for expressing human thought and philosophy, Dr. Zoé-Obianga noted how the colonialists oppressed local language, depriving the oppressed people of the depths of their mentality. Noting the lack of classes in the organization of most African languages, she argued that there is not the opposition of pejorative connotation one finds in the following oppositions:

> French—il/elle
> English—he/she
> German—er/sie
> Spanish—el/ella

Looking at her own background in the Pahouin group, Zoé-Obianga finds three principles worthy of examination: the cohesion of the group with a covenant of mutual responsibility both between kindred and with God; the protection of the individual whereby the group owes every individual man, woman, child, including old persons, love and support; and the emphasis on the better welfare of all. The participation of both women and men is a duty and a right recognized by all—*I am because I participate*. She sees the challenge to the Christian community to go beyond the traditional elements in the culture which afford renewal and to widen the horizon beyond the family or tribe of the Pahouin society. The voice of women, she says, has made possible the present awakening of conscience and she challenges men and women to act together, for history teaches us "that nothing is accomplished without courage and obstinacy."

Another African educator, Beatrice Luyombya, had told Niederaltaich participants that African tradition stressed human wholeness. She echoed what Julia Campos said about the Christian stress only on spiritual salvation in Latin America. Many churches in Africa, she said, overemphasize this aspect "as if persons could be compartmentalized into the Greek trichotomy of body, mind, and soul. This compartmentalization is unknown and totally alien to traditional African thought," she added. A person should be treated as whole, well aware that one part affects the other. "It does not make sense to preach the gospel of salvation in unpalatable condition." And she cited the starving people of Karmonja: "There is no need to give them another unworldly message which does not meet their conditions. People are not only spirit, they are body and mind; they therefore need food, security, and education as well as the gospel of salvation."

Mother Teresa

6

Scripture in
the New Community

Men and women who struggle with the role of Scripture in building the new community find themselves face to face with both the source of oppression and the source of liberation. In its interpretation on every continent, both in everyday use and in self-conscious study groups, Christians give their answers to such questions as:

Are Paul's statements on what women can and cannot do corresponding to our church's teaching? Are they still relevant today?

How did the attitude of Jesus toward women differ from the common religious and cultural view of his day?

How did the Genesis accounts affect your understanding of the man-woman relationship? How do they affect church teachings?

Can we develop language and images to describe God as both male and female? Are there qualities of God better described with female imagery? With male imagery?

The Sheffield section report stressed that the task of biblical interpretation is that of the whole people of God, not only of professional elites or experts. This approach is reflected in the report of the section's work which is filled with testimony and interpretation by the participants. Addressing both the context in which Scripture was written and its contemporary applications, they discovered that the Bible, though written in a patriarchal context, has antipatriarchal passages of great depth. Acknowledging that Scripture has been misused in some times and places to perpetuate social injustice and reinforce oppression of women in social contexts different from that in which the text was written, Sheffield found that what is universal and valid is that faith in Jesus Christ *is* new life. The new community of the gospel belongs to every age and generation in a new way. What is new in our time is the growing awareness of the full status of women and its implications of full personhood for both women and men. It is not the

59

meaning of the texts, past and present, that is at stake but their false use as authority and as justification for attitudes and actions that are against gospel revelation.

At Sheffield the argument that the Bible "speaks for itself" was countered by an African woman who said, "The Bible spoke for itself on the slavery issue for years. When the economy changed and large numbers of slaves were not necessary or profitable, consciousness changed, and people began to read the Bible differently."

"No act, attitude, or system of oppression can be properly legitimized by the reference to Holy Scripture or by appeal to its authority. It is incompatible with any confession of faith in the Lord Jesus Christ as God and Savior according to the Scriptures," the section declared.

The area of language, imagery, and symbols is fraught with controversy. In the preliminary study reports, a group from Finland wrote, "We cannot understand the necessity for raising the issue about the identity of God. Christ came in history as a man and taught us to pray: Our Father Who Art in Heaven. From childhood the image of God the Father, Heavenly Father, has been with us. However, now being adult, we can also understand God as person, who encompasses both sexes. Human beings as men and women are in his image. We have no need to change our current language. Although we speak about God the Father, we understand him as Spirit, a secret, which nothing human, male or female, can describe."

From Denmark came a warning: "The Bible does use female metaphors when it talks about God; the breast-feeding mother, the hen which gathers its chickens. We should, however, be aware not to identify 'soft values' with female God. If it is 'soft' to love, to care, to forgive, how can we begin to understand that these are human values?"

When the talk turned to imagery for God, an Asian man noted the importance of feminine qualities such as mother love, inner peace, and concern and said such qualities traditionally associated with women must be nurtured in men as well. A Danish woman commented that it was common for preachers to use male imagery in their sermons, such as weapons of war, to symbolize strength of faith. A man from Taiwan told that God was referred to in another religion as parent.

A North American Orthodox woman explained that the terms Father, Son, and Holy Spirit were not meant to connote masculinity but to lead to correct concepts about the Trinity. "All human terms are inadequate to express the transcendent, ineffable Godhead but Jesus Christ gave us the word *Abba* as an insight, not a block, and it is not easily to be exchanged."

The Sheffield section on Scriptures asserts that Scripture is addressed to persons created in the image of God, male and female in community, not to men or women exclusively.

God takes sides with the oppressed, they agreed. "We cannot speak about a new community of women and men as long as injustice to women prevails. We must not in the name of universal love conceal injustice. Rather we must act justly in order to effect love. In a community of men and women without justice, there can be no true unity."

Women Interpret Scripture

Two powerful and quite different ways of interpreting Scripture were experienced at Sheffield. There was a memorable sermon by Pauline Webb, an official of the British Broadcasting Corporation and a former executive of the British Methodist Mission Society. There was radical and rigorous Bible study led by an American theologian, Phyllis Trible, in which the Genesis account of creation, the Book of Ruth, and the Song of Songs were seen afresh. Strong examples of women interpreting Scripture were dominant image and reality at the international consultation.

Pauline Webb spoke at an ecumenical service in the Sheffield cathedral. "A chance to change and build a new community of women and men where 'all shall be well,'" the service booklet for that occasion begins. On a soft summer evening while it was still light, women and men from the Sheffield area joined with participants to see young people enact a chancel play, to hear the words of the English saint Julian of Norwich, and to hear a sermon by a woman. Public speaking and preaching are no new things to this woman who was formerly vice-chairperson of the World Council's powerful Central Committee. A preacher's daughter, Pauline has spent much of her professional life writing and talking on church matters. For her own church, she has been both an interpreter and a mission executive working primarily with churches in Africa and the Caribbean. She has a vast network of women and men friends in the community of the church across the world. Presiding over a mostly male group of clergy leaders of the World Council from time to time, and being thrown into situations like the visit of Pope Paul VI to World Council headquarters in Geneva, this is a woman accustomed to exercising a legitimate place in the world of both church and society. Today Pauline is in charge of religious broadcasting overseas for the British Broadcasting Corporation.

For the Sheffield cathedral service Pauline chose the text John 20:15 "Woman, why are you weeping?" which she described as the very first words which the risen Lord spoke to his church. The preacher pointed to a report recently released in Britain on pressure points in the lives of women and men. Men are likely to break down because of work-related failures, frustrated ambition, defeat in competition. But in the majority of cases of breakdown or severe depression in women, the causes could be traced back to the ending of some relationship.

"Some would say this is all because of our conditioning in our sex roles. Men are taught from the beginning they must succeed in their careers. Women are taught to invest their whole careers in loving and nurturing others. So for a woman a broken relationship can mean a broken heart. There seems nothing left to live for. So Mary stands in the garden weeping, believing that her relationship with her Lord has now come to an end. She has stayed beside him right to the last moment, even the moment of death. And now she has come to do what she can do to tend his dead body. No man would do that. In the culture of her time, tending to a corpse would be regarded as an act of defilement, fit only for a woman to undertake."

The preacher points to the irony that the only people we know actually to have handled the earthly body of Jesus were women who were at his birth and death, at his cradle and tomb. And yet, she says, the only people not allowed to consecrate the sacred elements of his body and blood are, again, women. And behind the prohibition lies deeply hidden the fear that somehow the female image brings defilement into the holy place. Here is how Pauline sketches the scene of Mary at the tomb, when she discovers they have taken the body of the Lord: "And, like many women, from whom that body is withheld, she almost gives up the search. But he seeks her out, 'Woman, why are you weeping?' he asks. She doesn't recognize him at first. Her eyes are too blinded by the tears to see the wound she has watched the soldiers inflict. But then he speaks to her by name, Mary. And here is the first great truth that comes out of this text for us: *Jesus speaks to each of us by our own name.*"

Pauline Webb comments on the importance of naming in the Christian tradition. Our Christian name given to us in baptism is written in the Book of Life, not our family name. And yet, she reminds us, many women hardly ever hear their own names used. And she confesses that when she goes on preaching tours where she has been given hospitality over a weekend, she often finds she has never heard the wife's name. "I've often never been told what it is. David introduces me to 'my wife.' The children all call her Mother, the neighbors speak of her as Mrs. Smith, but who is she? What is her name?"

This search for our unique identity can be very lonely and frightening. "So for Mary, standing there alone in the garden is indeed a terrifying experience. Then she hears Jesus speak to her by name. And her first instinct is to hold him fast. Then come the even more surprising words of Jesus, 'Do not cling to me.' He won't allow the woman to be fettered, even by her love for him. She must be free to be herself."

Instead Jesus sends the woman to join the community and gives her a message to communicate. "Go and tell my brethren." And she notes that the community of the church was defined even then in male terms because the men had gathered themselves in one place apart but Jesus sends the woman to bear the Good News. Would they believe her? "After all, what authority did she have? Only the authority of her own experience of the risen Lord. And that is all the authority we need," our preacher tells us. "That could give her the courage to go and join the new community which is about to be born, where the Spirit would be poured out on men and women alike and where sons and daughters would prophesy."

Noting how all the great announcements of the gospel

came through the lips of women, from the annunciation to the resurrection, Pauline says women have been "gossips" of the gospel throughout history. Defining "gossip" as one who tells good news, she finds it is a terrible indictment that the word has come to mean one who spreads bad news instead. She reminds us of the Orthodox sister who tells us how the gospel was spread to Georgia through the "gossiping" in the good sense of St. Nina. "And all of our histories can tell of women who have spread the gospel in a variety of ways."

Drawing from her vast experience in the ecumenical movement, the Englishwoman leaves us with a succession of vivid images of women: courageous women in the square in Buenos Aires, Argentina, making silent protest as week by week they await news of missing relatives; women in Chile making brightly colored collages depicting their situation and the social injustice of the land; South African women bundled into police vans and drowning out the sirens with the sounds of freedom songs. "Or go to Australia and listen to the aborigine women telling the legends of their 'dreaming time' which warn of underground monsters which may destroy the earth if they are disturbed, in the very area where men are now mining for uranium."

Calling on her congregation to communicate the gospel together in the community as a sign that the new order has already begun, she asked for sharing in the traditional teachings and new insights, "the authenticity of scholarship and the authority of experience," witnessing to the gospel of liberation not just for women but for women and men and the whole creation.

A Love Story Gone Awry

Perhaps the most astringent and controversial part of the Sheffield experience was the intense and, to most, totally different interpretations that biblical scholar Phyllis Trible brought to the conference plenaries. This scholarly woman with a deep appreciation of the thought-forms and poetry of the Old Testament set about her task with notable linguistic, literary, and hermeneutic skills. There was nothing glib about the presentations but much that was astounding to women and men in this new approach to the Bible. North American delegates were perhaps more prepared for this kind of feminist interpretation and were most comfortable with it. While a great many delegates expressed the opinion that they would have preferred to have Bible interpreters from a variety of church backgrounds and cultural experiences, few faulted Trible for being unable to command their attention.

As Mary Tanner described it to the Faith and Order Commission at Lima, these studies were detailed in scholarship, based on a thorough knowledge of Hebrew text, and relentless in the concentration required from those engaged with her. She drew us into new ways of viewing Genesis 2 and 3, the Book of Ruth, and the Song of Songs from a woman's perspective. "Without exception people were spellbound that those patriarchal narratives which had subordinated women for so long should be interpreted so differently on the basis of the Hebrew text and the new techniques of scholarly analysis." Far from drawing from contemporary idiom or example, Dr. Trible delved deep into the culture, language, style, and context of biblical times to come up with totally new and usually startling interpretations of the ancient stories. Her approach, in addition to the tools of biblical and literary criticism, included insights from feminism and psychology.

Describing her technique in her book *God and the Rhetoric of Sexuality,* Dr. Trible wrote, "Within Scripture, my topic clue is a text: the image of God male and female. To interpret this topic, my methodological clue is rhetorical criticism. Outside Scripture, my hermeneutical clue is an issue: feminism as a critique of culture. These clues meet now as the Bible again wanders through history to merge past and present" (p. 23). To attempt to paraphrase or partially quote these studies which are tightly reasoned and have astonishing conclusions is to do a disservice to Trible and her method. In her book the study of Genesis 2–3 takes some 70 pages and includes detailed literary criticism of the form, intimate knowledge of Hebrew, wide-ranging wit, and deep intelligence that cannot easily be suggested by snippets of quotations.

In her interpretation of the Garden of Eden story, the Union Theological Seminary (New York) professor describes not the first man but the first earth creature. (She argues that this first creature was initially sexually undifferentiated.) Knowing this text is the basis for much of the stereotypical thinking about woman as helpmate (though the Hebrew word does not mean assistant), temptress, betrayer, Trible tells us that the serpent and the woman discuss theology. Cunningly, the serpent asks, "Did God really say you shall not eat from every tree in the garden?" According to Trible, the response of the woman is intelligent, informative, and perceptive. "Theologian, ethicist, hermeneut, rabbi, she speaks with clarity and authority" as spokesperson for the human couple. The woman has stated well what Yahweh God requires. Her uncompromising words of obedience are the very center of scene two. "Yet the center cannot hold. The serpent challenges, indeed refutes the logic of obedience, claiming for himself absolute knowledge of life and death." The woman contemplates the tree and finds it appealing. She doesn't discuss it with her man—she takes, eats, gives. The man played no part. He does not theologize. "Instead his one act is belly-oriented and it is an act of acquiescence and not of initiative. If the woman is intelligent, sensitive, and ingenious, the man is passive, brutish, and inept."

Trible is not excusing either. "Having exceeded the limits of life, this couple has destroyed its harmony. Instead of fulfillment, joy, and gift, they now experience life as problem which *they* must solve; as threat which *they* must eliminate, and shame *they* must cover up." As Trible sees it, where there was once mutuality, there is now hierarchy of division. The man dominates, the woman is corrupted in becoming slave, and the man is perverted in becoming master. "His supremacy is neither a divine decree nor the female destiny. Both their positions result from shared disobedience.

"Life," she says, "has lost to death, harmony to hostility, and fulfillment to fragmentation and dispersion. Male and female have violated creation and creator." What do we say to this tragic ending? Trible hopes that having heard the story anew, we need no longer accept traditional interpretations that proclaim the subordination of female to male as the will of God. "Rather than legitimizing the patriarchal culture from which it comes, this story places that culture under judgment and thus can function to liberate and not enslave us."

There is a chance to change offered by the story, Dr. Trible concluded. It tells us who we are (sexual creatures of equality and mutuality). It tells us who we have become (sexual creatures of oppression). "So it opens up possibilities for a change, for a return to our true creaturehood under God. It calls upon us, this very day, female and male, to repent."

The Name of God

When Moses asked for the name of God
he received the answer: I am that I am

Let us also say this ourselves
Say: I am that I am
Say it twice, three times . . . ten times
Feel it, eat it, let it stream through
Your whole body, let it become truth in you

Let is shape you and reshape and
renew you and grow in it.
Say it tomorrow again, because you
will be anew, who you are
but may be different from now
and yesterday.

Go outside and hear the trees
rustling it, the birds singing it, the
grass saying silently: "I am that
I am" and say it with them.

And when it is truth in yourself,
turn to your neighbor or your
child or your husband or wife or
any fellow human being and say:
You are that you are and
I am that I am
You don't need to be as I want you for me
and I don't need to be as I think
that you expect from me . . .
or as you expect from me.
I am that I am and you are that
you are

A great breath will come into us
We don't need to *prove* that we are something of value
We don't need to achieve this or that
before we may *be*:

I experience my full identity
I meet you in your real dimension
of mystery

This is BE-ING
We salute each other in this room
of freedom that is called LOVE

I bear the name of God
and *you* do
And what *happens between* us
is the un-speakable name of God

From which the human world
continuously renewing itself
comes into *being*.

Elizabeth Streefland
The Netherlands

Sister Madeline Marie Handy, Cameroon

photo by Jo-Ann Price Baehr

7

The Third World
Speaks Out

To delegates from the Third World, the Sheffield plenaries, with their emphasis on the role of women in the church and the strong input from North America and Europe, had two major failings. They concentrated too much on what they considered to be Western perspectives and preoccupations limited to the church. They failed to address the relationship of women's oppression to racism and economic oppression. True, Father Tissa Balasuriya had raised the interrelationship of sexism, racism, and classism, but the overwhelming majority of voices during the first four days spoke the languages of the West and except for the West Indian general secretary of the World Council of Churches, a Roman Catholic priest from Sri Lanka, and an African woman, they were European and North American. Africans, Latin Americans, Asians, persons from the islands of the Pacific and the Caribbean were growing restless. Orthodox from the Middle East did not share the concerns of women from North America and Europe.

The restlessness erupted at the meeting of concerned Third Worlders on the fourth evening. Evenings were deliberately left free in order to care for concerns that emerged and for the participants to get to know each other in informal settings. Following the morning plenary the next day, the frustrations that the concerns had little relevance to "who we are" and "where we come from" were presented to the group in a formal statement from Third World participants. In a brief but powerful statement they said that to speak of women and men in the church only is an unnatural separation of the church as an arena for relationships between the sexes within the overall societal contexts of their countries. "This kind of separation is unnatural also because it speaks only of a minority of women and men like most of us, who want to be recognized as equals in terms of being qualified to minister to fellow Christians *within* the church.

"As representatives not only of the church but also of our particular societies, we feel we cannot confine our concerns to speaking of wholeness and community within the church. There is a large struggle for the realization of human wholeness, for liberation from widespread oppression that is classist and racist, and in this struggle our sisters and brothers from other faiths are caught up as well. . . . A more essential reason for exploring the nature of a new community of women and men within the church is to grow into a renewed, redeemed, and redeeming community within this global context of desperate struggle against exploitation and poverty, hopelessness, and despair."

Charging that the plenaries had not provided sufficient input on and exploration of the global context, they pleaded for the sections and discussions to take the larger liberation struggle into consideration. Geographical and financial realities, they said, had prevented adequate Third World sharing and search for common conclusions in advance of the meeting. They reminded the consultation that economic and political power of First World nations affected the "everyday life of sisters and brothers deeply and unremittingly. . . . Any gathering of women and men in community in the church, if it is to be prophetic, caring, and ministering, cannot and dare not ignore this fact." They asked specifically for time to be set aside for regional meetings and that sectional groups keep in mind the global context of struggle for all their work.

The cry for recognition was heard and profoundly affected the outcome of the conference. The first reaction was a hurried meeting of the conference leaders at the coffee break and a decision that the next period would be set aside for the requested regional meetings. The meetings were held with a strong confessional and penitential note in those of North America and Europe and more expressions of frustration and outrage on the part of the Third World. Wisely, all agreed that listening to each other and working together on a broader agenda was the way to solve the problem. In the North American area meeting which I attended there were numerous expressions of sorrow, guilt, and, from those not usually exposed to Third World concerns, some considerable shock. Rather than drafting a rhetorical expression of corporate guilt, the Americans opted for listening and learning and engaging in a common search.

"We say to women of the First World: 'Sisters, take care that your tax dollars are not killing our sons and husbands,'" a Latin American woman warned. She spoke of the all-powerful police in her country, the system of torture in the prisons, and added, "Sisters, it was your money which is contributing to this. Wake up to your sins of commission! Bring pressure on your senators. We have no voice of our own."

A woman from South Africa expressed fear that the participants from the First World were feeling, "'OK, let them blow off steam. They'll be OK.' How can we glibly speak of community any time we speak of the powerful and the powerless? We are not here to inflict pain for itself—we are here to be a voice for the voiceless.

"What would happen if you got the ladies from the kitchen to come and sit here? Would even they have the priorities we hear from the First World?"

And Deborah Belonik, a delegate of the Orthodox Church in America, wondered whether the technique of "You say your theology and I'll say mine and we'll see who gets points on the screen" was to be the style of the consultation. A British woman desiring ordination in the Church of England asked if the Roman Catholics and the Orthodox would use the "bludgeon of unity" to prevent the ordination of women. Yet another participant wondered why so little had been said about the many women who felt oppressed by the overwhelmingly male language and imagery of the liturgy and predicted that unless this was changed many women would leave the church.

Such was the atmosphere when participants began to settle down seriously to their work in sections. There had been two meetings of the sections prior to the Third World statement. The serious work of the conference involving recommendations and future directions was done in the eight sessions of the sections.

Every ecumenical study conference I have attended has similar problems—a relatively short time span for people from vastly different cultural and theological backgrounds to come to grips with problems, explore their differences, find some common agreement, and articulate that common understanding in the form of conclusions that will speak to the churches they represent and to the World Council itself. It isn't easy and Sheffield did as good a job as most.

Worship and Bible study, formal occasions such as the reception by the lady mayor of Sheffield at the Town Hall, the cathedral service at Sheffield Cathedral following an excursion to York, and regional meetings were interspersed with the four formal plenary presentations on the crowded agenda. Meal and tea times became the occasion for what little relaxation there was. World Council of Churches meetings have been called statement factories and the style of the Sheffield meeting was in that tradition. Some at the consultation felt that the style was too much in the male pattern of the past and should have allowed more participation in plenaries. After formal presentations there were questions and comments from the floor, but these are always somewhat formalized simply by the fact that they must be translated.

Third World participants would have preferred a fuller debate of the issues they raised in the total group but by the time their concerns were introduced the consultation was on the section track. Some felt the structure oppressive and inflexible. Others felt it was necessary in order to keep the obligation the meeting had to provide material to be acted upon at the Central Committee and the Faith and Order Commission. Despite all these divergences about theory and practice of meetings, the group took the Third World challenge seriously in the sections and produced an enormous amount of work. Again, as at other meetings, it varied in quality and sometimes plastered over wide splits in belief with vague rhetoric. All in all a remarkable amount of solid work was done which will challenge the ecumenical movement for the remainder of the century and beyond.

The seven sections were divided into groups of between twenty and thirty persons (observers, press, stewards, and staff were welcomed to the meetings but the final vote was by official delegates). Sections faced with huge questions like authority and church structure divided into subgroups of half a dozen or so persons. Drafts were submitted first to the total consultation. This is a slow and laborious process but it is highly participatory. This style gives everyone an opportunity to comment on everything. Because the World

Council of Churches includes such a wide spectrum of theological belief, sometimes there is no consensus. At Sheffield this was true of the question of the ordination of women. There was more consensus on political justice and freedom than on the role of women in priestly ministry.

Christian Revolutionary Change

Later in the meeting the Europeans shared a written response which expressed gratitude for the Third World's emphasis on specific problems in their own struggle for liberation. While admitting that "we have not listened early enough to your cries for justice in the Third World," the Europeans said, "in personal encounters and by listening we have discovered you." They expressed themselves also as dissatisfied with the economic system that put the Third World in bondage and was "rigid, alienating, oppressive, and destructive."

The truth was that few in any region were satisfied with the current world economic and political order. The Europeans felt they must launch more effective programs in their own setting to help people understand the interests, mechanisms, and consequences of the old economic order. They expressed determination to battle militarism and racism, aware that they had been able to do little to interpret the World Council's Program to Combat Racism in their own churches.

While North Americans and Europeans might muster two cheers for democracy, there were barely any for the economic system that exploits the Third World and contributes to dehumanization everywhere. "We are learning how intimately related our problems are. Sexism, racism, and classism depend on the way our societies are organized and ruled. We challenge ourselves with the radical question of whether our social system must not be completely changed, aiming at a new system that sees peace and social justice as indispensable. Our Christian faith encourages our conviction that our world can be changed. We feel called to participate in this Christian revolutionary change," the Europeans declared.

The basic awareness of sexism as interwoven with other oppressions is everywhere evident in the sections and the recommendations at Sheffield. How did the Third World participants feel they were understood? By the time of the final plenary they prepared a response to the responses. They found some leaning over backward and insisting on a Third World viewpoint on everything. "Others have remarked that the statement was a brief flare-up and has died a quick and proper death," they said. They found solidarity, indifference, and some paternalism (maternalism was not mentioned). Rather than dealing with the issues in sections as the consultation process had planned, they would have preferred to give more plenary time to these enormous issues. The fact that the majority (80 percent) of the responses sent to Geneva to the study itself were from North America and Europe might have been a tip-off that the questions as expressed were not of the same urgency and priority in the Third World.

Did this mean that the Third World was unconcerned about sexism? No, those delegates answered. They are grateful for the awareness, noting that in the two-thirds of the world they represent women are the most exploited people on earth. While they share an experience of life that pushes beyond sexual discrimination in the churches, "we affirm with our sisters in the First World that we share with them the common experience of being subjugated, controlled, and exploited within the large context of our countries. But when we began to share our experiences we were forced to see beyond our noses because behind those men who dominate with their so-called superiority, we became aware of a faceless, formless beast holding them by their skinny throats, threatening and making objects of us all, women and men. We had to ask, 'What can we do?' " Here they admitted that as Third World Christians they too are a privileged minority. "We Christians in the Third World . . . exploit and oppress. We grow fat from the labor of thousands. Our rich women make slaves of our unfortunate sisters. We share in the guilt of dehumanizing. . . . " And they pressed that this process of dehumanization is not only allowed but encouraged in the name of progress and the pursuit of life, liberty, and happiness.

The final statement presented by the Third World as prologue to the section reports asked for an end to the exploitation of the powerless by the powerful wherever that is found "whether it be power appropriated through the presence of hormones, hard cash, or hair color." And they ended with a statement that there is increasing urgency especially for women as the nurturers of life to gather in strength to stop the mindless proliferation of nuclear and other arms that is a threat to life. The Rev. Dr. Albert Aymer, a Jamaican on the faculty of Drew Theological Seminary, Madison, New Jersey, had an opportunity to view the consultation from two angles. Named by a U.S. church, the United Methodist Church, he met with the North Americans in their frustrating search for a proper response to the original Third World statement. But as a West Indian he also took part in the deliberations of the Third World. He said Americans were unsure how to respond to the linkage of the three oppressions. "We are caught up by a sense of failure." Europeans, he felt, didn't seem to have the same problem and thus were able to respond with a written response to the Third World plea.

It is important to know that the European group included those from a variety of economic situations—state socialism of Scandinavia, communist Eastern Europe, poorer countries of the south, the industrial giant of Western Germany, and the ailing capitalism of Great Britain, to mention a few. The North American group included a handful of Canadians, including a Roman Catholic from French-speaking Quebec, and a shameful overwhelmingly white delegation from churches in the United States. There was no official woman delegate who was Hispanic or black. The Rev. Jackie Grant from the African Methodist Episcopal Church, who commented following Father Balasuriya, was present as an observer. Albert Aymer from the Caribbean represented the United Methodist Church and Bishop Frederick Talbot the African Methodist Episcopal Church and that was it! Not one single U.S. church named an Asian American (an Asian observer was present), Hispanic, or black woman who was able to attend. While there were many excuses (persons asked and unable to come), there was the overwhelming reality that this did appear to be a white, middle-class, even academic, women's subject. Men were mostly clergy.

A white American woman who is on the Faith and Order Commission of the World Council of Churches characterized the conference as a time when new voices were heard which haunt us with their pain. "The struggle for the true community of women and men will never be realized until powerless people become true partners whose gifts are recognized as needed to complete the whole community." The Rev. Jeanne Audrey Powers, a United Methodist ordained woman who has been proposed to be a bishop in her church and declined to stand for election, said that "when new voices that have been silent for centuries share their pain, the new community breaks through. The Western male system is being dismantled by the power of the new partnerships. The church is being empowered by women and men together in new ways. Sheffield symbolized all of that."

A Demonic Symphony of Oppression

Third World concerns are present in much of the Sheffield material but it was in the section on freedom and justice, chaired by an American, Dr. Letty Russell, that these concerns had the strongest focus. More concerned with society than inner workings of church life, this group saw the struggle for change as one struggle. Racism, sexism, classism, and all other forms of domination and rejection are linked together "in a demonic symphony of oppression."

Father Tissa Balasuriya, OMI, director of the Center for Society and Religion in Colombo, Sri Lanka, had introduced the idea of what came to be known as the "web of oppression" in an address in which he traced the relationships between the search for equality and new community in the church and the secular movements for liberation, particularly as they relate to women. A well-known Roman Catholic theologian with special interests in liberation theology and eucharistic theology, Father Tissa sounded themes which would reverberate throughout the conference.

A common feature of sexism, classism, and racism is the tendency to regard the others not as free, responsible persons or human community but as objects, things to be used for another's pleasure or profit, the Roman Catholic theologian asserted. The evidence points to class as a main dividing line and contradiction in society, Father Tissa said. However, the emancipation of the workers or an oppressed race did not necessarily mean a triumph over male domination, he warned. Similarly, antisexism alone does not ensure freedom from race and class domination. What then is the goal of Christians? Integral human liberation as promised by God through Scripture, he answered.

In race and class relations the basic demand is for justice and dignity. In the relationships of women and men more is demanded in understanding, sharing, and love, Father Tissa observed. "The liberation and fulfillment of one is inextricably linked to the liberation of the other. These dissimilarities make the domination and movements of liberation concerning the sexes a different kind of complexity from those concerning race and class."

Father Tissa said that in Christianity, Jesus gives an example of unselfish love for others that offers a higher ideal quite harder than merely fighting for one's rights. "For the follower of Jesus, participation in the struggle for human liberation from oppression of all types should be the normal, the minimum for a decent human life. . . . " In following Jesus, struggle against evil and oppression is inevitable. Religion can help to humanize revolutionary struggles for liberation and social change can help purify religions, he said.

"Our goal has to include a radical transformation of the structures of society, even at the international level. A vision of a just, participatory, and sustainable society cannot be made real without a redistribution of land and resources among the poor peoples of the world. The future of humanity requires an end to the arms race, to the despoiling of nature, to the running down of the world's nonrenewable resources, and requires more simple life styles especially among the affluent. Such change will not be easy and the tasks of integral human liberation will require much suffering by those committed to do it."

In holding up a vision of a holistic approach to integrated human liberation, the Asian Christian challenged us to transcend the limitations of our ghettos and evolve a common loyalty to the total human cause and the care and destiny of our planet and universe. New world economic order is essential, he said. But he also realized that in relations of women and men the personal conversion is essential and primary. In this sense, the women's struggle can make a contribution to the permanent and ultimate transformation of persons to accept the other in her or his otherness. "Insofar as this is realized, we approximate the society freed of oppression and exploitation, and build on human understanding of the new community of women and men, i.e., the substance of the kingdom of God on earth."

Spirituality the Wellspring

This appeal to spirituality as the wellspring of activity on behalf of freedom and justice is stressed in the report of the section on justice and freedom. "We understand racism, sexism, and classism as both personal and collective manifestations of sin," wrote Section VI. "The evils of our time—sexism, racism, and classism conflicts—cannot be explained only by reference to cultural and economic factors or to social and political structures. Each of these plays an important role in human life.

"But the roots of our struggles are illumined by the biblical concept of sin. Therefore, it is an illusion to believe that the root of evil has been eliminated by the institution of a new order. Instead our struggle for justice and freedom must be unceasing. . . . The struggle against evil in our hearts and in our world has to take place on the personal and the social level. We must begin by asking for the gift of repentance."

It was with this clear-eyed view of the struggle which Christians must wage that the section on freedom and justice prefaced its work. Noting that the principalities and the powers that rule our lives and the world must be faced together, the report warns against being divided and working against one another. At the same time that the struggle against oppression is universal, it is acknowledged that the struggle can be very particular as well. We each must take up the struggle for change against the oppression that is forced upon us in our situations. For the starving, food is the first step on the road to freedom. For the rich, actions to betray their own class and stand in solidarity with the poor is the first step. . . . Persons and groups oppressed are oppressed in different degrees. The document points out different cases. A black woman in South Africa oppressed by racism, sexism, and classism will find her first struggle against racism though sexism and classism are linked with it. A woman in Guatemala may find herself oppressed by imperialism, classism, and sexism. Her first struggle might be against imperialism, yet the other struggles must go hand in hand. A white woman in the middle class is oppressed by sexism yet her struggle is also linked to classism and racism.

International tourism and accompanying prostitution was chosen as an example of oppression that is both universal and particular. A shocking list of exploitation of women, teenage boys, and even children was offered by the section. Young girls are sold in "marriage" to visiting men and often end up as servants or prostitutes. A visitor to a refugee camp in Thailand noting the absence of girls above eight is told they have been sold into prostitution. Powerful tourist agencies are accused of offering local girls as part of a travel package in Thailand, Tahiti, and the Philippines. Women's groups in France have made an inquiry into these services but have found it difficult to collect evidence as no offers are openly made. In countries surrounding South Africa tourist business conducted by white South Africans offers sexual activity across racial lines.

8

Beyond Sheffield

Women and men at Sheffield distilled their thought and convictions into seven densely typed pages of recommendations forwarded to the units of the World Council of Churches and its Central Committee. The recommendations to various units of the Council such as Justice and Service and Faith and Order met with no major obstacles, but one proposal to the Central Committee which met the following month in Dresden, East Germany, proved a bombshell. The committee of 125 policy-makers debated whether there should be equal representation of women and men on the World Council's committees and commissions. A number of men spoke strongly in favor of the proposal. But what seemed to some a simple matter of equality of representation proved quite another matter to others who considered that the Council would supersede its authority in dictating to the churches against their inner beliefs. The issue touched sensitive nerves in the Orthodox world which already had major questions about the nature of their participation in the World Council in the eighties. It was perceived as more than a difference about the role of women. There were underlying questions of authority, biblical understanding, and doctrine.

In the context of a worship service with voices of the broken community articulating findings from all parts of the world, the preface to the presentation of the report from Sheffield to Dresden stressed that this study was not another program against sexism or even for more participation by women but about *women and men* becoming human in the new community and how to bring that about. The context was not illness but health and healing—not brokenness but new community. These brave words may overstate the actual case but the emphasis had been on women and men working together. One of the difficulties is that while it was intentional that more women than men should participate in the study, an alarmingly small number of men actually saw this emphasis on working together as a matter of priority of interest on any continent. Nonetheless, what happened at Sheffield was a mutual discovery by women and men of a vision of new ways they might work together in the church and world.

The Central Committee heard how the study had attempted to deal with Scripture in the new community, with justice and freedom in the new community, and identity in the new community. Orthodox leaders argued that their understanding of membership in the World Council varied sharply from the proposal for equal representation. Deeper than the question of whether there were trained and qualified women in Orthodoxy to serve on the decision-making groups was the issue of whether the World Council could prescribe to the churches how they should choose their representation. The debate raged for parts of several days and in the end a compromise resolution presented by a young American woman, Jan Love, which affirmed the principle of equal representation of women and men, was adopted. The Orthodox mostly abstained or voted against the resolution even though it was emphasized that it was not establishing a quota or mandating compliance but suggested a goal or criterion.

The intensity of the feeling about the recommendation extended also to the letter addressed to the churches. Normally such letters to the churches gain blanket approval and are transmitted to the churches without any demurrals. But the letter from Sheffield was faulted by the Orthodox at several points: for what it said about the ordination of women and for what it said about sexuality. It also was called into question because it invoked the Holy Spirit, a characteristic common to such letters, and to most rhetorical utterances of church people. The letter had said, "What did we in Sheffield hear the Holy Spirit saying to the churches?" Under a section entitled, "We gained perspectives," the letter held "that for many women and men there is real pain . . . where, for instance, women feel called to the ministry of word and sacraments and ordination is not open to them or where the Church has not responded to creative developments in society." Another passage that was ambiguous to some concerned a statement rejoicing that "sexuality is not opposed to spirituality, but that Christian

spirituality is one of body, mind, and spirit in their wholeness." Opponents did not like this letter going out to the
churches with general endorsement. They felt it was subject
to misinterpretation, particularly in churches where ordination of women to priesthood is against the dogma of the
church. Again a compromise was reached in which the
general secretary was instructed to send the letter to the
churches with the complete report outlining the debate
which occurred in Dresden.

Planners of the study were not discouraged by the debate,
nor were those who were theologically and ecclesiastically
informed about the World Council of Churches surprised.
Most agreed that it was healthy for the Council to confront
head-on issues which had been present in the Council since
its inception but never openly debated at length in its policy-making group.

When the results of the community study, including the
recommendations, were presented to the Faith and Order
Commission in Lima, Peru, at the beginning of 1982, a male
Orthodox professor and two women teachers who had
shaped the study were the principal speakers. The Faith and
Order Commission of the World Council of Churches is that
unit made up almost exclusively of professional theologians
whose work is to overcome the theological barriers to the
unity of the church. This work existed before the present
World Council of Churches came into being and joined with
the movement called "Life and Work" to form the World
Council in 1948. Lima was the occasion for agreement on a
profoundly important study called "Baptism, the Eucharist, and Ministry," which offers a framework for a possible
reunion of the churches. This landmark document is obvi-
ously the event that historians will associate with Lima.
Two other significant studies, one on the Apostolic Faith
and the other on the Unity of the Church and the Renewal of
Human Community, are areas where the community study
is to be "infused."

Professor Nicholas Lossky challenged the assembled
theologians to take the community study seriously and incorporate it in all the reflections of Faith and Order. He
suggested that any reflection on the divinity and humanity
of Jesus Christ should also consider the figure of the blessed
Mother of God as a female prototype in the ecclesial com-

munity. And he suggested a variety of ministerial roles, aside from the question of the priesthood and presiding at the Eucharist:

Some ministries are perhaps mysterious, secret ones. But the visible ones are more numerous than appears (because we have often neglected or even prevented them). According to the nature of our conception of the Church, all laity, men and women, are responsible for the faith and its expression in the liturgy and life. Women can therefore fulfill many functions (sometimes they do; often they do not for reasons of neglect or sinful historical circumstances).

Among functions of responsibility and authority may be quoted the positions in church administration, in parish or diocesan councils; women can be lay members of synods. Women can teach in the church: many in the church's history have evangelized, done missionary work (several have been canonized as "equal to the Apostles"); catechism is often their special province. They can fulfill liturgical functions; reading, singing, choir directing. . . .

More important to my mind: many, especially in recent decades, have become iconographers. This is a very responsible position for in traditional orthodoxy an iconographer is no mere painter or decorator, he or she is a responsible theologian. Iconography is the visual expression of the Church's common confession of the faith. An iconographer is therefore called upon to be as much of a theologian as a Father of the Church. And if women can be iconographers, why should they not hold chairs in theological academies in "noble" subjects (not only "subsidiary" ones) such as Dogmatics, Church History, Canon Law, Liturgies . . . ?

Why not recognize the possibility of restoring forms of a feminine diaconate for women? Not, of course, just for the sake of a sort of concession to feminist demands, but wherever the necessity is felt for the good of the Church (in some countries where adult baptism is more and more current, this would perhaps be very necessary).

In conclusion, we must *very* seriously take into consideration the challenge presented by the study on "Community of Women and Men in the Church" and not make it a separate study but incorporate it in all our reflection in Faith and Order. It is obvious that if we accept the ministerial function of every member of the Church, this must not cease to find expression in the Baptism, Eucharist, Ministry reflection of the member churches. Our striving toward a common expression of the Apostolic Faith cannot avoid, at least in commentary form, a reflection on the eucharistic community and its responsibilities. This same reflection, particularly on the divinity and humanity of Christ, must envisage a consideration of the figure of the blessed Mother of God as a female prototype in the ecclesial community.

Arguing that reflection on ministries should be conducted with two things in mind: that all have a gift of the Spirit, a *diakonia*, and that specifics are not abolished but overcome, Professor Lossky did not sidestep the issue of ordination of women to the priesthood and presiding at the Eucharist. "The absence of such ordination in our tradition has to do with the maleness of Christ. In Orthodox liturgy, the bishop [priest] is at certain times regarded as image or type of Christ," he explained. "This is no mere allegory; typology or symbolism in the Orthodox tradition is no mere imagery, no mere evocation of another reality. A symbol is not merely something suggested, it is participation in the true reality, the disclosing of God's plan, of the eternal in the transitory, the discovery of 'the point of intersection of the timeless with time' [T. S. Eliot, *Four Quartets,* Dry Salvages, V]."

The meaning of this symbolism needs deep theological reflection, he said, along with the meaning, implication, and place of the maleness of Christ, together with the absence of female "presidents" of the eucharistic community in the tradition. "Such a study has not been made yet. It will probably take a long time. But meantime be patient with us and give us the possibility of effecting this reflection."

In a reflection on Lima entitled "In Sight of the Top: Faith and Order at Lima," Michael Kinnamon said that there is no doubt that the community study is one of the most talked about programs in the World Council. "There is little doubt that it has directly touched more people, encouraged more grass roots participation, during its brief four years of existence than any other Faith and Order-related study."

Two women professors of theology, Letty Russell, of the Yale Divinity School, and Mary Tanner, who taught at the Anglican Seminary in Cambridge, spoke to the impact of the study at Lima. Dr. Russell, a Presbyterian minister, spoke of searching for a new language of life that speaks for the whole life of the community of God's people. Women working in groups across the world have called for a new life in the face of death. "For women especially, who give birth to life, the life of community is the only life possible. As those in the study have viewed the forces of destruction and death on every side, they did not come up with one new paradigm of our death-dealing world—both North and South, East and West. They challenged through all their reports and questions the paradigm of domination in all its death-dealing and oppressive elements. They added their voices to their suffering brothers and sisters everywhere and the very voice of groaning creation itself to call for a language and interpretation of reality that brings the sacrament of life into the midst of death."

Recalling the view offered in the North American consultation of the pyramid of authority (domination) against the paradigm of doxology, Dr. Russell spoke candidly about the difficulty of women and Third World groups when their perspectives did not fit in the pyramid structure of systematic theology. "The price exacted to fit in is loss of their own perspective and culture to 'good theology.'" In the traditional theological world, the tendency, she said, is to view discussion as a competition of ideas all aiming to gain the top spot and vanquish others. "In our search for unity, there are other initiatives possible in which women and outsiders present a chance to change.

"The problem of women in ministry might also become a possibility for a new theological understanding when the paradigm of reality is doxological, looking for ways to share in the praise of God through participation of all the people of God in the common ministry of Jesus Christ on behalf of all humanity."

Dr. Mary Tanner, currently an ecumenical officer of the Church of England, focused on interpretation of Scriptures, an issue in the community study. Whatever the subject chosen for study—identity, roles, sexuality, patterns of ministry—it always came back to use and abuse of Scripture, the nature of biblical authority, and the tasks of biblical interpretation, she said. What became quite evident was that the same Bible which is used to limit the self-understanding of women is also the source of hope. Women and men are now rereading the Bible, with fresh eyes, discovering how texts, written by men in the patriarchal age, translated and preached by men for 2,000 years, can be read and used in ways that point almost exclusively to a new inclusive community.

The Continuing Agenda

In summing up the relation of the Faith and Order Commission to the report of the community study, Michael Kinnamon reflects that there was both broad and deep appreciation but evident relief that it had gone "beyond a feminist critique of inequality in the church to a search for new forms of partnership and community." Lima's formal comment was put this way: "We affirm the full partnership of women and men in the quest for unity. Any future unity across confessional boundaries would be belied by continuing barriers and forms of discrimination within the community of the church." But, Kinnamon confesses, underneath this surface link between unity and renewal the controversies still rage.

"What, for instance, constitutes sexual discrimination? Some churches, to take the best known example, oppose the subordination of women, but refuse to ordain them on doctrinal grounds. Faith and Order must face the implications of such a stance for unity among Christians," Kinnamon writes in *The Ecumenical Review* (April 1982). He lists the issues which remain central to Faith and Order: the significance of the representation of Christ in the ordained ministry, the evidence in Scripture and tradition for participation of women in the church, the way in which various structures of authority in the church help or hinder the search for renewed community, the question of what it means to be human in the image of God, and the problems of language, imagery, and symbols of God in worship and theology. This formidable list constitutes an agenda for the men and women engaged in Faith and Order.

No longer a separate study of the World Council of Churches, the search for the new community of women and men must be conducted in all of the aspects of the Council's work—the Faith and Order unit where it was lodged, the women's department—all the units of the World Council which have specific recommendations to follow up on. Among the decisions of the Central Committee were that all World Council publications adopt inclusive language and that the Council set up procedures to monitor and evaluate its own work in regard to racism, sexism, and classism. Women's concerns will be incorporated into all World Council justice and service programs focusing on women who are refugees, migrants, prisoners, or disabled. On the long list of recommendations from Sheffield, careful reference was made to appropriate Council units for follow-up. Neither the issues nor the persons of both sexes concerned about them will go away.

A New View of Authority

The World Council does not legislate for member churches. Ultimately the questions of authority and structure must be faced by the churches themselves. The Sheffield section dealing with these questions made it clear they are not simply seeking to replace one power group with another of another sex. The search is not for a rigid, authoritarian power on the male model of history but a new model that utilizes skills and leadership learned by the powerless. Current church structure often alienates persons. Power was seen not as possession, control, command over others, but the ability to implement action and obtain effective results. Power defined as ability to implement change and respond to human need must be shared power.

This vision of a leadership model based on the model of Jesus, the Christ, was offered:

—sharing of money and resources.
—creating an open and inclusive atmosphere of learning and solidarity.
—living the gospel and witnessing in society, considering all people as worthy of dialogue, of revelation, of health, healing, and forgiveness.
—standing for justice, liberation, and peace.
—using structures to serve people, not people to serve structures.

Are there any such models, one might ask? At Sheffield, examples given included the Aladura Movement of Nigeria, the Sojourner Movement in the USA, the women's movement in various parts of the world, basic communities in Latin America and Europe. Collaboration and teamwork were seen as signs of the new community.

The chance to change is offered not only to councils and denominations but to women and men wherever they are.

9

Reality to the Vision

To counter millennia of oppression of women and centuries of male dominance in the churches, the efforts of two hundred persons at an international consultation may seem paranoid or at best pitifully small. But recall the thousands of others who have already participated in the struggle, the formal acceptance of the consultation's recommendations by the important World Council of Churches Central Committee in 1981 and at the Faith and Order Commission in Lima in 1982. Add the reforms likely to come at the Council's forthcoming Assembly in Vancouver in 1983, along with changes that are taking place in member churches on every continent, and the picture looks less bleak.

Most important in any movement toward new community is what happens in the minds and hearts of people. To gain some understanding of the possible future, we addressed three questions to Sheffield participants at the conclusion of the conference. We asked:

1. What has been the most valuable learning or experience from this conference? Were there any revelations, surprises?
2. How will the learnings affect the future of the community of women and men in your situation?
3. And what do you consider the major obstacles to achievement of a true community of women and men in the church?

There was a surprising unanimity of response. To many in the Western countries, the awareness of how Third World people feel about issues of economic justice, human rights, and peace came, if not as a surprise intellectually, with a decided emotional impact. Women from affluent countries coming with sharp consciousness of their oppression as women found that this oppression was imbedded in many other forms of oppression for their Christian colleagues in the Third World. A man from Switzerland put it this way:

"For me the most important learning experience was the widening of the horizon by exposure to different contexts in which the question of a new community of women and men was placed. The statement of the Third World was crucial in this experience and forced me to form a clear concept of 'humanization' in which I myself need to place the question in my own context."

An Orthodox woman from North America said Third World participation "enlightened me about their particular feminist problems which do not relate to North American feminist concerns." A woman from Singapore felt that heightened sensitivity to others' needs, values, and how much they differ "even though we share the same Lord Jesus" was a principal insight. Her discovery was that "we're all in the web of oppression and express our power through classism, sexism, and racism, and that the root cause is our individual and collective sin." A participant from Latin America found "a precious experience in being able to communicate with many persons of different manners and to work, think, and argue different profound and vital themes with persons of different countries, races, and cultures."

The lived experience of the new community of women and men, referred to in the letter issued by the consultation to the churches, is mentioned again and again as a foretaste of what the new community *could* be. "Sharing the pains and the concerns and the joys was something great. I appreciate the whole atmosphere where I could feel the harmony in diversity," a woman from India said. "But I was surprised and shocked to see the phases we are passing through in the liberation from sexism and the utter helplessness of the churches which seem to close their eyes against the dehumanizing life styles which come in the name of freedom," she added. "I deeply share the concern we expressed towards the victims of this liberation process and hope the new community will become a reality."

Some surprises weren't so pleasant. A New Zealand delegate was shocked at the political "game playing." "I, in my innocence, had not expected it at a World Council conference. The implied threat of withdrawal from the World Council of Churches, for example, whenever anything unacceptable to the Orthodox church came up, sad-

dened me." An Orthodox participant remarked that the
Orthodox Church in America would feel "more and more a
different religion and separatist if other churches in the
ecumenical movement adopt some of the feminist proposals
at this conference."

A "missionary kid" who grew up in Japan found the First
World/Third World clash the source of deepest impression.
The young woman from the United States was "devastated
by Third World people who spoke of painful alienation from
their own culture because of a religion that somehow linked
them with the privileges and oppressive systems of the
West. It was noted that I'd never considered such ideas
before. As a teenager I wrestled with the implications of
cultural imperialism. And it's not that I accept at this point
in my life an overly simplistic picture; a caricature of missionaries as the wicked destroyers of other people's pure
cultures. I think what was painful and fruitful about the
week is that old memories were reawakened of how hard I
had to battle my dad for the freedom to think my own
thoughts rather than swallow his theology whole. And
didn't I hear those same battle sounds echoing in the voices
that spoke at the mike. I remembered being lost between
two cultures, not really an American but hardly Japanese
either. Do my Third World Christian friends also wander
lost in their dreams through the marketplaces of the city?"

Unlike some who warmed to the cry of "racism, sexism,
classism," this young woman felt it had a cold and manipu-
lative ring to it. Yet she responded deeply to the struggles of
individual women—of one from Africa or another from the
Philippines and others. While rejecting the "ugly rumor that
self-centered spoiled American feminists care only about
their own status, salary, and prestige," she added a post-
script of confession to an African sister, "No, I don't know
what it's like to starve to death."

A man expressed a different fear: "I learned that the fear
of being beaten by women is only a fear based on male
ignorance and prejudice. Rather, we (both sexes) are strug-
gling in spirit of ourselves to draw each other into a more
human existence. This certainly requires us to be frank, to
live with each other's anger, to listen, and to change. I was
delighted that the strong feminist tone of the early days was
balanced by the intervention of people from developing

countries and again that each listened to the other in the effort to create a full community."

An Englishwoman found most valuable the experience of receiving into oneself the motions and judgments of those whose people had suffered and are suffering from white male Christian domination and then "gently with them to examine whether such judgments are still valid when applied to our generation and if so, to see what we must do to redress the wrongs."

Perhaps most surprising to Third World delegates, at least mentioned most often by those who responded to the question, was the form of the Bible study. Phyllis Trible's scholarly reversal of the usual interpretation of Old Testament texts shook the foundations for some. A Latin American questioned whether it would not have been better to have besides this kind of interpretation a view from the vantage point of liberation theology. "Are we not too much preoccupied in bringing new Bible interpretations, one more perfect than the other, when more important is that we do not give enough attention to the praying, the thanksgiving, the hearing of the Holy Spirit?" "The Bible study was a revelation. Few of us from Sri Lanka have heard of the new perspectives given us by feminist theologians." This woman found the Bible study interesting, but "what really moved me was Pauline Webb's sermon in the cathedral. I have learned quite definitely that, whatever the external differences, we women are sisters under the skin."

One summary read: "I learned that process is more valuable than product. That new revelation is possible from interpretation of the Bible. Surprised by joy that women and men in the church can experience each other in faith and love." Some who did not think they were capable of reflecting theologically found that they had something to contribute which was valuable to the group. Over and over again came delight from both sexes that they had experienced a new community in which women and men were equal and valued participants. One mentioned the community of Ecclesfield where the Sunday morning visit during the conference had been an experience of full community of women, men, children—"an experience of lively community full of warmth and joy" in a local Anglican congregation.

For many the most valuable experience was in the groups and small sections and subsections where talking, listening, understanding many different persons and traditions underscored the commitment to the church and to Christ. "I particularly appreciated the opportunity to learn and understand more about the Orthodox Church . . . even when I found it difficult to agree with what was being said," a woman from Scotland recalled.

At every ecumenical conference there are young persons known as stewards who do much of the hard menial labor of conferences for the privilege of being present. At this particular consultation, stewards were welcomed to express their opinions and to contribute to the preparation of reports.

One young man expressed surprise that Sheffield still depended so much on European and North American participation at plenary presentations. "Apparently lay people, women, youth, the Orthodox, and Third World people still need to continue to plead for proper recognition. We still haven't reached the stage where we are automatically given space and time to speak. It would have taken a very naive person not to have expected a statement to come from Third World participants during this lopsided consultation." With revolutionary ardor, he advocated doing away with all the hierarchy, officialdom, protocol, gold print, and red carpet. "We must begin to overcome our separations, to eliminate our hang-ups and our double standards, and especially to work at peeling off all our thick layers of hypocrisy. We must get our priorities straight, reconsider the way we use our time, the way we spend money." Another delegate was shocked at the male model of process during the conference, with heavy concentration on plenary presentations delivered from "above," orientation toward a product (recommendations and reports), and reliance on expertise and experience.

Perhaps the significant thing about the response to the encounter is that so many experienced the same emotions and thoughts despite differences in age, theology, sex, or geography.

Rocks in the Road

There was an astounding degree of agreement on the major obstacles to the achievement of true community of women and men in the church: the way the world is organized, the sins of the past, and the sins of the present. Amid the fears and uncertainties of this world, one delegate said, women and men are looking for security in everything from rigid sex roles to stockpiles of nuclear weapons. Named among the sins of the past were "women who have been burnt by men, now leery of any sort of joint venture; women who have been made to feel second-rate being afraid and unable to speak freely and responsibly before men; men who have always had women leaning on them now unable to give up control."

A man put it even more bluntly: "Lack of example to overcome a certain castration fear on the part of men (not physical of course) and intimate relationships with other mechanisms of self-defense (economic and political)." The self-image of men as businesslike, soldiers, and athletes (physical, mental, and emotional) was seen as a major obstacle. Again and again patriarchy of society and church, tradition, and church structures were listed.

Fear. Fear of change, fear of women by men, fear of women in the ordained ministry, fear that women in decision-making offices in the church will threaten women in the home. The fear, often hidden, of women's sexuality, together with the suspicion on the part of women that all men want to keep them under. Fear. Fear. Fear. This was the word most often mentioned as the major obstacle to creation of the new community.

A man mentioned the obstacles afforded by language and symbols of prayer and liturgy which exclude women and the way lectionaries do not include a balance of readings affirming women. Another major stumbling block is Western education's appalling emphasis on reason, academic achievement, and competition and the assumption (until recently) that this is the province of the male. The corollary is the "equally appalling" neglect of the emotions and creativity which are considered female . . . all of which has had a catastrophic effect on much of the life of the institutional church and the interpretation of the gospel. The sins of selfishness and lack of love were frequently mentioned along with bigotry, traditional ways of thinking, insensitivity, lack of openness to the Holy Spirit, male enjoyment of power and authority, women's complicity in their own oppression, stereotype of male/female conduct, rigid church structures.

Under "personal prejudice" one woman ended with a kind of credo: "Every person, female or male, black or white, homosexual, married or single, divorced or remarried, has the right to be a fully participating member of Christ's family on earth. There should be no prejudice because of race, color, sex, creed, or personal life styles. I am a First World white married woman in a happy partnership with my husband. I expect that partnership to last until death do us part. But I will not discriminate against anyone whose situation is different from my own. Christ did not do so."

An Orthodox woman asks, "True community, according to your standards? It will never occur. But according to our standards, we need more publications educating women as to cultural taboos and customs. We need to rethink the question of deaconesses. It will take time and money."

Hope and Home

Despite a depressing catalog of obstacles, the delegates to Sheffield revealed an enormous amount of hope that change is possible and that the conference could affect the community of women and men in their respective situations. "I hope I can convey a message of Jesus Christ, the hope of the world, women and men together. I tend to be a liberal, skeptical, questioning Christian. The fact that a symbol of the whole world has managed to live together for a whole week with some degree of harmony amidst differences has made the Christian ethic in this troubled world of ours a much more powerful concept for me" (New Zealand). An Anglican deaconess from the United Kingdom, commenting that the reality of community as an experience is its own justification, added, "I suppose I return with renewed determination not to steamroll the opposition but to listen more attentively."

Speaking from her background in the Mar Thomas Church of India, a delegate said that the challenge lies in reinterpreting these ideas into "more acceptable forms. Even that will create chaos, but I hope the new order will surely come out of the chaos." There was little cheap optimism expressed but a great deal of faith-rooted hope. A

woman from the Netherlands commented that other forces
are also at work to change the male structure and forms and
experiences at Sheffield will help her to articulate better to
male colleagues some of the difficulties of the church structures in which she works.

A man from Australia said the consultation will have no
effect at all unless "those of us who were there do something and even then it is difficult to work on issues except in
small groups of people." He saw that the Anglican Church
in Australia will receive encouragement to continue its slow
movement toward the ordination of women but thinks the
whole structure of the church must be reexamined as recommended by the consultation. "Recommendations need
to go to the right people in each member church, not just to
the archbishop's desk."

A candid assessment from North America, while ap-
preciating the model offered by the consultation of inclusion
of men in the study without having women give up leadership roles, was pessimistic. "Outside of myself the impact
will not be great. There are few people in our church who
eagerly wait to hear the voice of the World Council of
Churches on any issue." A Swiss pastor told of his own
conversion to more education in his parish. He intended to
assign the issue higher priority and change language in
worship services, sermon topics, church seminars, and
other aspects of congregational life.

To a Roman Catholic participant the search is not for a
new community but for the one that existed at the beginning
of the Christian church—where each loved the others as
themselves. The recovery of this community could mean
happy, but painful, growth for Christianity, not only for
individuals, or our families, but for the whole society. From
Asia came the comment that in Singapore the problem is not
to get more women in the church decision-making bodies
but to persuade men to serve at all and to offer training to
persons of both sexes.

In Sri Lanka, it will be difficult to introduce the new
concepts because of a "strong streak of fundamentalism"
with absolute literal interpretation of Scripture running
through all the churches. This woman foresaw strong opposition to any introduction of Sheffield perspectives from
young people as well as old. "It will take courage to speak of

these things but it will have to be done." She proposed to take insights gained from the consultation to a newly established commission on women of her National Christian Council.

Perhaps a steward put it most forcefully when he wrote, "Such a reference to my own context immediately reminds me of the weakness of my own position, of my own hypocrisy, which consists of traveling to Sheffield in search of a new community, whilst doing nothing whatsoever in my own church or home town." Hence, he concluded that he is one of the obstacles to the new community and has no right to speak unless he changes. And he pointed to a communications difficulty experienced by a woman steward who failed to understand the combination of words which were the consultation theme. "The title I understand, the words I understand, but it's what I see that I can't understand." Like some Third World delegates, he felt that the community of women and men in the *church* was too limiting—it should be church and world. "But that's the same thing as the *oikumene*—the whole inhabited world."

A New Ecclesial Reality

Connie Parvey, in addressing her colleagues on the World Council's Staff Executive Group following Sheffield, recalled the original confusion about which group in the Council should take responsibility for the study—the Faith and Order unit which deals with theological questions or some unit dealing with human rights. In 1976 the Central Committee of the World Council had debated whether the whole question of the role of women in the church was a matter of unity or human liberation. "What we realized at Sheffield was that unity and human liberation cannot be separated. . . . We need an ecclesiology that brings these elements together not because it makes good theory but because it reflects the reality of our ecclesial life."

Ecclesial reality may sound unreal to those who do not know ecumenical jargon or the special language of theologians. Actually it is a term that has come to mean something that has the marks of a church but isn't what we have ordinarily classified as a church. For example, the term came into vogue (if one could consider the somewhat arcane discussions of theology in an ecumenical setting vogue) in a

discussion about the nature of the World Council itself
when the churches came together in the ecumenical setting
of the World Council of Churches. The Council is not a
church but a fellowship of churches yet in its life there is
something which has ecclesial reality.

In summing up Sheffield, Connie recalled Zoé-Obianga's
oft-quoted "I am because I participate." Sheffield, she said,
became an experience where "we are because we participate." The particular way in which persons participated at
Sheffield helped both the content and the style of the meeting beyond what its planners might have envisioned. Other
groups have learned this among the poor in Latin America
when the ecclesial life belongs to them and is taken by them.
Similar events and experiences have changed the nature of
the black church in the USA and black churches in South
Africa, she said.

"We discovered at Sheffield that who participates makes
a difference. To the surprise of many, we were not divided,
women and men against each other, but we discovered in
the search for new community a common framework for our
endeavors." And she speculated on what would happen if
the two-thirds women and one-third men formula were
applied to the Dresden meeting of the Central Committee
where the ratio is more like nine men to one woman.

The meeting was a first, its principal organizer claimed, in
that it was neither business as usual nor a women's meeting
but a common searching of women and men with women in
the majority for the first time ever in an ecumenical movement, and probably the first time ever for a church meeting.
Here we might pause and comment that the intention is not
to reverse the tables and seek to have women outnumber
men in all church settings but to come nearer to the goal of
having true partnership. A cynic might observe that many
men who were present were there because they were known
to be in favor of partnership and as such were not representative of the real power-holders in the church. Whatever the
motivations for the Sheffield mix, the group, after quite a bit
of debate, has suggested that in the future the advisory
committees of the World Council be composed of an equal
number of women and men. To set the stage for such a
revolution, the group asked that half of the speakers at the
Vancouver Assembly be women.

"We are not talking about entrance into power or taking over power, but creating more power in order to empower, to vitalize, to share," Ms. Parvey said. The most significant common discovery of the consultation for most participants was that you cannot separate church and society and talk about them as though they were two different realities. "The Christian community is part of society, but not just a reflection of society. It is a critic, an 'as if' community, a prophetic community that seeks to live a vision and, in so doing, experiences both its risks and its joys. It is from this context that it views ministry and ordination: the church as a church for others—not an ethnocentric church."

For Sheffield undertook no less a vision than the transformation of the church, its structure and its power directed to service of people in the world. "We discovered that the new ecclesial community is evangelistic. It does not look inward but outward. The work on ministry, church structures, and Scripture are all examples of this," Connie reported. She spoke of prophetic ministry that grows out of the needs of people, in conflict and dirtying its hands in such societal issues as the abuses of prostitution, economic disorder, and the search for peace. The recommendation on the diaconal ministry is oriented to this serving view: to ministries of healing, of service, of care, and prophetic witness.

The new ecclesial reality of ordained women was not faced as some would have liked at Sheffield but the reality was there in the presence of 20 to 25 percent of the official participants who were ordained women. "Their presence is an ecclesial reality, a fact. It cannot be made invisible." Actually it was the archbishop of Canterbury who raised the question most prominently at the meeting even though his church does not ordain women. There was sufficient concern that the question was not being raised out of ecumenical courtesy to those churches which do not ordain women. A statement was read on the last day of plenaries that the reality not be ignored (see pp. 46–47).

Ms. Parvey declared that the new ecclesial community looks for resources for renewal within tradition—the capital T Tradition in the church, traditions in various communions, and cultural traditions. "The mark of the new community of women and men is not that it is a 'creation out of nothing' but it looks for its counterparts in history and culture and in the depths of ecclesial experience, past and present."

The new ecclesial community validates the "God-given experience of women, not women as the invisible backbone of the church, but like any good backbone, visible. As Koreans say, 'strong-boned' women."

A new ecclesial reality will be just as difficult to communicate, understand, and achieve. That term will not be used by ordinary women and men as they seek the new community. But when they experience it, they will know something of the reality of the wholeness God intends for faithful people. Meanwhile those who search may be considered a bit odd, difficult, annoying, uppity, heretical, foolish, or whatever the culture and church of the time and place decree. As they experience the marks of the new reality they will be sustained in their quest.

Women in Exodus
Commune with God

God in heaven and on earth
greater and vaster than all humans.
You are more than our father,
for we have experienced

Luke 11:11 that fathers can give us stones
Matt. 7:9 when we ask for bread.
You are more than our mother,
for we have experienced
that mothers can disown us
when we become ourselves.

You are not the God of the old church
where a few men rule over all of us,
where their language reveals
that they have never included us,
that we have only been used
to establish their empire
which has never served You,
but the masters of this world.

So we live in this strange land
with phallus-symbols that frighten us:
rockets, cannons and guns.
And they still tell us
to bear children
to people our nation.
That's not how You meant Your Word:

Gen. 1:28 "Be fruitful and multiply!"

Now we have emigrated,
and we experience a new community in the desert
where we learn to be ourselves,
where we experience You uninhibited
as the God of a New church,

where there is neither Jew nor Greek
nor bond nor free,
nor male nor female
Gal. 3:28 but all ONE in Christ.

You will put down the mighty from their seats,
and put them before the lion
and tell it
to protect them.
And when their fear is over,
their hatred of all those
     who think differently,
     who pray differently,
     who speak differently,
     who act differently,
     who feel differently,
     who love differently.
And when their hatred is over,
they will no longer care about power,
because they will have discovered LOVE,
and Your Kingdom will really begin.

Helen Schmidt
Germany

Eucharist—Zimbabwe

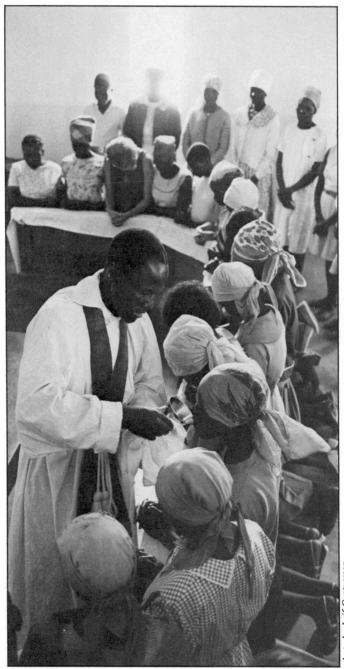

A Letter from Sheffield

Sisters and Brothers in Christ, we long that you may hear us, for we belong together with you in the Church and in a common humanity.

Brothers, can you not hear the "sighs too deep for words" of women who suffer war, violence, poverty, exploitation and disparagement in a world so largely controlled by men? Sisters, can you not see how the lives of men have been trapped by the effects of their having this power and a supposed superiority?

We speak as those who have been seeking to listen anew to Scripture and to live the tradition of the Church in its many forms. Thus we have heard a word of God for today about a vision for our human life—a renewed community of women and men. We speak with urgency. In a world threatened by nuclear self-destruction women and men are made more sharply aware that they need a new partnership as equals before God; in churches and societies which men have dominated in ways deeply damaging to women and to men, we need both repentance and faith to move forward at God's call through the gospel.

What did we in Sheffield hear the Holy Spirit saying to the churches?

We learned:
— how deep are the emotions involved in any reflection on our being as women and men;
— how hard it is to address and envision God in ways that respect the Christian understanding of personhood rather than suggesting male superiority;
— how great is the need for education on the issues of our consultation;
— how radical may be the changes needed in our societies.

We received:
— a foretaste of a global community of women and men

vulnerable to the pain of all forms of oppression and united in struggle against them.

We gained perspectives:
— seeing that for many women and men struggles against tyranny, militarism, economic exploitation and racism are the immediate task;
— that Christians in many places need to call on governments to overcome exploitation, particularly where women and men have become victims of wrong patterns of development, through cheap labor, migrant labor, or tourist-orientated prostitution;
— and that for many women and men there is real pain in the frustrations of a church life controlled by male leadership, where, for instance, women feel called to the ministry of word and sacraments and ordination is not open to them or where the Church has not responded to creative developments in society.

We recognized:
— the importance of including Christians from every continent and culture and from all churches in this Community Study in order to achieve a perceptive hearing of all concerns.

We rejoiced:
— to recognize that sexuality is not opposed to spirituality but that Christian spirituality is one of body, mind and spirit in their wholeness.

We sang at Sheffield:
— the Magnificat of Mary that celebrates God's liberating intervention; the praise of Jesus in whom we look upon the human face of the Triune God.

We invite you to pray with us:
Eternal God, as you created humankind in your image, women and men
male and female, renew us in that image:
God, the Holy Spirit, by your strength and love comfort us as those whom a mother comforts:
Lord Jesus Christ, by your death and resurrection, give

us the joy of those for whom pain and suffering become, in hope, the fruitful agony of travail:

God, the Holy Trinity, grant that we may together enter
into new life, your promised rest of achievement and
fulfillment—world without end. Amen.

Sisters and Brothers in Christ, we long that you will join us
in giving reality to the vision which we have seen.

Notes

Except where books are specifically referred to in the text, all the quotations come from the preliminary documents, the working documents made available at Sheffield, and the Sheffield section reports. Some speakers may think that I have made omissions, quoted out of context, and juxtaposed their texts. They will be correct. My purpose was to give the substance and the flavor of the meeting as I experienced it. I have tried to deal fairly. Those who wish to know more are directed to the full report. Poems were spontaneous expressions of consultation participants. Several were read at the closing worship.

Preface

Constance F. Parvey, ed. *The Community of Women and Men in the Church* (Philadelphia: Fortress Press, 1983). The official text, this volume contains all plenary addresses, section reports, and other significant documentation.

Susannah Herzel, *A Voice for Women* (Geneva: World Council of Churches, 1981). A history of the role and status of women in the World Council of Churches, with particular attention to the department related to women.

Introduction

Philip Potter, "A Chance to Change," opening address, Sheffield Consultation.

Chapter 1

Potter, "A Chance to Change."

Chapter 2

Constance Parvey's account of the Community of Women and Men in the Church Study is included in the report of the Asian Consultation held in Bangalore, India, in August 1978 and the report of the African Consultation held in Ibadan, Nigeria, in September 1980.

The poem included on page 29 is from *The Journey from Sheffield to Dresden* (Geneva: World Council of Churches, 1981). A report on the Sheffield Consultation made at the Central Committee, World Council of Churches, Dresden, East Germany, August 1981.

"Marriage, Family, and Life Styles in New Community," Section IV Working Paper, Sheffield Consultation.

Chapter 3

Elisabeth Moltmann–Wendel and Jürgen Moltmann, "Becoming Human in New Community," plenary presentation, Sheffield Consultation.

Elisabeth Behr–Sigel, "Orthodox Tradition as a Resource for the Renewal of Women and Men in Community," plenary presentation, Sheffield Consultation.

Nicholas Lossky, speech introducing the Sheffield Report at the Faith and Order Commission, World Council of Churches, Lima, Peru, January 1982.

Chapter 4

Authority and Community in Christian Tradition (New York: National Council of Churches, 1981). Study document of the Faith and Order Commission, National Council of Churches in the USA.

Robert Runcie, "Community of Women and Men in the Church," opening address, Sheffield Consultation.

Kathleen Bliss, *The Service and Status of Women in the Churches* (London: SCM Press, 1952).

Constance F. Parvey, ed., *Ordination of Women in Ecumenical Perspective: Workbook for the Church's Future,* Faith and Order Paper No. 105 (Geneva: World Council of Churches, 1980). It should be read by those interested in the subject of ordination to the priesthood. It comes out of the pre–Sheffield international consultation and is intended to deepen the dialogue in churches.

"Ministry and Worship in New Community," Section III Working Paper, Sheffield Consultation.

Chapter 5

Jean Baker Miller, "The Sense of Self in Women and Men: In Relation to Critical World Questions," plenary presentation, Sheffield Consultation.

Bliss, *Service and Status of Women.*

Towards a Theology of Human Wholeness (Geneva: World Council of Churches, 1980). Report of the Niederaltaich Consultation held at the Niederaltaich Abbey, West Germany, September 1980.

Rose Zoé-Obianga, "Resources in the Tradition for the Renewal of Community," plenary presentation, Sheffield Consultation.

Chapter 6

Questions such as those quoted are used in the preliminary study. Those who wish to engage in this kind of exploration are urged to get the study book *Community of Women and Men in the Church* (New York: Friendship Press; Geneva: World Council of Churches, 1978).

"Scripture in New Community," Section I Working Paper, Sheffield Consultation.

Pauline Webb, "Woman, Why Are You Weeping?" Sermon
    preached at Sheffield Cathedral during the Sheffield Consulta-
    tion.
Phyllis Trible, Bible studies at Sheffield Consultation. All quotes
    are from the Sheffield document. Trible's Bible studies were
    based on her book *God and the Rhetoric of Sexuality* (Philadel-
    phia: Fortress Press, 1978).

Chapter 7

Father Tissa Balasuriya, OMI, "Women and Men in New Com-
    munity: Insights from Liberation Struggles," plenary presenta-
    tion, Sheffield Consultation.
Third World Statement and European Response, mimeographed
    documents distributed at Sheffield Consultation.
"Justice and Freedom in New Community," Section VI Working
    Paper, Sheffield Consultation.

Chapter 8

Minutes of the Central Committee, World Council of Churches,
    Dresden, East Germany, August 1981.
Minutes of the Faith and Order Commission, World Council of
    Churches, Lima, Peru, January 1982.
Nicholas Lossky, Letty M. Russell, Mary Tanner, plenary pres-
    entations on community given at the Faith and Order Commis-
    sion, World Council of Churches, Lima, Peru, January 1982.
Michael Kinnamon, "In Sight of the Top: Faith and Order at
    Lima," *The Ecumenical Review* 34, no. 2 (April 1982).
"Authority and Church Structures in New Community," Section
    V Working Paper, Sheffield Consultation.

Chapter 9

All quotations from participants here are from interviews and a
    questionnaire prepared by the author and distributed at the
    Sheffield Consultation.
Constance F. Parvey, "Report on Sheffield Consultation for Staff
    Executive Group," World Council of Churches, September
    1981.

Bibliography

1. Scripture

Russell, Letty M. *The Liberating Word: A Guide to Non-Sexist Interpretation of the Bible*. Philadelphia: Westminster Press, 1974.

Stendahl, Krister. *The Bible and the Role of Women: A Case Study in Hermeneutics*. Philadelphia: Fortress Press, 1966.

Trible, Phyllis. *God and the Rhetoric of Sexuality*. Philadelphia: Fortress Press, 1978.

Wahlberg, Rachel Conrad. *Jesus According to a Woman*. New York: Paulist Press, 1975.

2. Identity and Relationship

Christ, Carol P. *Diving Deep and Surfacing: Women Writers on Spiritual Quest*. Boston: Beacon Press, 1980.

Miller, Jean B. *Toward a New Psychology of Women*. Boston: Beacon Press, 1977.

Russell, Letty M. *The Future of Partnership*. Philadelphia: Westminster Press, 1979.

3. Ministry and Worship

The Community of Women and Men in the Church Study. Bangalore Consultation, United Theological College, August 1978.

Hageman, Alice. *Sexist Religion and Women in the Church: No More Silence*. New York: Association Press, 1974.

Parvey, Constance. *Ordination of Women in Ecumenical Perspective,* Faith and Order No. 105. Geneva: World Council of Churches, 1980.

Weidman, Judith L. *Women Ministers: How Women Are Redefining Traditional Roles*. New York: Harper & Row, 1981.

4. Authority and Church Structures

Webb, Pauline. *Where Are the Women?* London: Epworth, 1979.

5. Justice and Freedom

Collins, Sheila. *A Different Heaven and Earth*. Valley Forge, Pa.: Judson Press, 1977.

Neal, Marie Augusta. *A Socio-Theology of Letting Go: The Role of a First World Church Facing Third World Peoples*. Ramsey, N.J.: Paulist Press, 1977.

Ruether, R. *New Woman/New Earth: Sexist Ideologies and Human Liberation*. New York: Seabury Press, 1975.

Russell, Letty M. *Human Liberation in a Feminist Perspective*.
    Philadelphia: Westminster Press, 1974.

6. Tradition

Julian of Norwich. *Revelations of Divine Love*. Translated by
    Clifton Wolters. Baltimore: Penguin, 1966.
Katoppo, Marianne. *Compassionate and Free: An Asian
    Woman's Theology*. Geneva: World Council of Churches, 1979;
    Maryknoll, N.Y.: Orbis Books, 1980.
Moltmann, Jürgen. *The Trinity and the Kingdom of God: The
    Doctrine of God*. London: SCM Press, 1981.
*Orthodox Women: Their Role and Participation in the Orthodox
    Church*. Report of the Consultation in Ayapia, Rumania, 1976.
Ruether, R. *Religion and Sexism: Images of Women in the Jewish
    and Christian Traditions*. New York: Simon & Schuster, 1974.
Sexism in the 1970's. Report of the West Berlin Consultation,
    1974.
Study on the Community of Women and Men in the Church. New
    York: Friendship Press; Geneva, World Council of Churches,
    1978.
Toward An Ecumenical Consensus: Baptism, Eucharist, Ministry.
    Faith and Order Paper No. 84. Geneva: World Council of
    Churches, 1977.